# 100 Math Brainteasers

# 100 Math Brainteasers

Zbigniew Romanowicz, Bartholomew Dyda

**Illustrations**
Jacek Skrzydlewski

**Cover design**
Pawel Kucfir

**English Translation and Adaptation**
Adam Fisher, Stephen Potocki

**Typesetter**
Andrzej Nowak

© Copyright by Tom eMusic
ISBN 978-1-62321-029-8
Tom eMusic

www.tomemusic.com
New York 2012

# Table of Contents

**CHAPTER 1 – NATURAL NUMBERS AND INTEGERS**

1. AT THE BOOKSTORE . . . . . . . . . . . . . . . . . . . . . . . 8
2. AQUARIUM . . . . . . . . . . . . . . . . . . . . . . . . . . . 8
3. MULTIPLYING THE SPOTS . . . . . . . . . . . . . . . . . . . 8
4. THE YEAR OF SOPHIE'S BIRTH . . . . . . . . . . . . . . . . . 9
5. I WILL NOT BE A TRIANGLE!. . . . . . . . . . . . . . . . . . . 9
6. A MEASURE OF SUGAR . . . . . . . . . . . . . . . . . . . . . 9
7. RIDDLE MAN . . . . . . . . . . . . . . . . . . . . . . . . . . 10
8. WHAT DID TOM WRITE?. . . . . . . . . . . . . . . . . . . . . 10
9. NINE-DIGIT NUMBERS . . . . . . . . . . . . . . . . . . . . . 10
10. PUPILS AND GEOMETRY. . . . . . . . . . . . . . . . . . . . . 11
11. WAX CLOCKS . . . . . . . . . . . . . . . . . . . . . . . . . . 11
12. A PECULIAR NUMBER SEQUENCE . . . . . . . . . . . . . . . 11
13. DOTS ON THE SIDES. . . . . . . . . . . . . . . . . . . . . . . 12
14. ABSENT-MINDED JOAN . . . . . . . . . . . . . . . . . . . . . 12
15. A MATTER OF AGE . . . . . . . . . . . . . . . . . . . . . . . 12
16. NEW YORK HAS THE UPPER HAND! . . . . . . . . . . . . . . 13
17. A CHOCOLATE PROBLEM . . . . . . . . . . . . . . . . . . . 13
18. KINGLETS. . . . . . . . . . . . . . . . . . . . . . . . . . . . 14
19. EVEN? ODD? EVEN?.... . . . . . . . . . . . . . . . . . . . . 14
20. GREAT CONTEST FOR AUTHORS OF MATH PROBLEMS . . . . . . 14
21. TOM AND HIS SEQUENCES . . . . . . . . . . . . . . . . . . . 15
22. SAYS AGATHA. . . . . . . . . . . . . . . . . . . . . . . . . . 15
23. ONE SESSION AFTER ANOTHER . . . . . . . . . . . . . . . . 16
24. DIGITS 'RESHUFFLE'. . . . . . . . . . . . . . . . . . . . . . . 16
25. REMEMBER YOUR PIN . . . . . . . . . . . . . . . . . . . . . 16

**CHAPTER 2 – DIVISIBILITY AND PRIME NUMBERS**

26. HOW OLD IS MR. WILSON? . . . . . . . . . . . . . . . . . . 18
27. MR. T'S SONS . . . . . . . . . . . . . . . . . . . . . . . . . . 18
28. MYSTERIOUS MULTIPLICATION . . . . . . . . . . . . . . . . 18
29. A ONE HUNDRED-HEADED DRAGON . . . . . . . . . . . . . . 18
30. THE POWER OF A WEIRD NUMBER . . . . . . . . . . . . . . . 19
31. A COLUMN OF PLASTIC TROOPS . . . . . . . . . . . . . . . . 19
32. THE MAID OF ORLÉANS . . . . . . . . . . . . . . . . . . . . 20
33. SPECIAL NATURAL NUMBERS . . . . . . . . . . . . . . . . . 20
34. INTEGER BREAK DOWN . . . . . . . . . . . . . . . . . . . . 20
35. DIVIDE NUMBERS . . . . . . . . . . . . . . . . . . . . . . . 20
36. THE MAGNIFICENT SEVEN . . . . . . . . . . . . . . . . . . . 20
37. NOSTRADAMUS AND HIS PROPHECY . . . . . . . . . . . . . . 21
38. SQUARE RIDDLE . . . . . . . . . . . . . . . . . . . . . . . . 21
39. MULTIPLY AND ADD, MULTIPLY AND ADD... . . . . . . . . . . 22
40. PLAY ON NUMBERS . . . . . . . . . . . . . . . . . . . . . . 22

**CHAPTER 3 – EQUATIONS**

41. ZERO-SUM GAME . . . . . . . . . . . . . . . . . . . . . . . 24
42. THE CHINESE AND THEIR BICYCLES. . . . . . . . . . . . . . 24
43. LONG JUMP COMPETITION . . . . . . . . . . . . . . . . . . 24
44. CALLING A SPADE A SPADE IN THE GARDEN . . . . . . . . . . 25
45. FAST CREEPERS . . . . . . . . . . . . . . . . . . . . . . . . . 25
46. CAKE LOVERS . . . . . . . . . . . . . . . . . . . . . . . . . 26
47. CHIP IN FOR A NEW BALL . . . . . . . . . . . . . . . . . . . 26
48. PRACTICAL JOKERS . . . . . . . . . . . . . . . . . . . . . . 26

49. HEAD START FOR DAVE . . . . . . . . . . . . . . . . . 27
50. QUARRELS ALONG THE WAY . . . . . . . . . . . . . . 28
51. A HARD NUT TO CRACK . . . . . . . . . . . . . . . . . 28
52. THE SMALLEST NUMBER OUT OF THREE . . . . . . . 28
53. SUM UP IN THE SIMPLEST WAY . . . . . . . . . . . . 28
54. WATERMELON HALVES . . . . . . . . . . . . . . . . . 29
55. BUNNIES FOR SALE . . . . . . . . . . . . . . . . . . . 29
56. VORACIOUS SHEEP . . . . . . . . . . . . . . . . . . . 30
57. MICHAEL THE PROFLIGATE . . . . . . . . . . . . . . 30
58. THE TWINS AND THE REST . . . . . . . . . . . . . . . 30
59. THE CASHIER'S MISTAKE . . . . . . . . . . . . . . . . 31
60. CLASS IN PAIRS . . . . . . . . . . . . . . . . . . . . . 31
61. ANNA'S AGE . . . . . . . . . . . . . . . . . . . . . . . 31
62. HOW OLD IS GRANNY? . . . . . . . . . . . . . . . . . 32
63. MUSHROOM GATHERING . . . . . . . . . . . . . . . 32
64. GAMBLERS . . . . . . . . . . . . . . . . . . . . . . . . 33
65. AM I THE POWER? . . . . . . . . . . . . . . . . . . . . 34
66. A USED UP WHEEL . . . . . . . . . . . . . . . . . . . 34

## CHAPTER 4 – GEOMETRY

67. ROADSIDE VILLAGES . . . . . . . . . . . . . . . . . . 36
68. DIVIDE THE TRAPEZOID INTO TWO . . . . . . . . . . 36
69. DIVIDE THE TRAPEZOID INTO FOUR . . . . . . . . . 36
70. CUTTING THE FIGURE INTO THREE . . . . . . . . . . 37
71. RECTANGLE OF SQUARES . . . . . . . . . . . . . . . . 37
72. A BIT OF WHITE, A BIT OF GREEN . . . . . . . . . . 38
73. THE CUTTING STRAIGHT LINE . . . . . . . . . . . . 38
74. CIRCUMFERENCES OF THE FOUR . . . . . . . . . . . 38
75. TRIANGLE NOT SO STRAIGHT . . . . . . . . . . . . . 39
76. A CLEVER SISTER . . . . . . . . . . . . . . . . . . . . 40
77. CIRCLES ON A TRIANGLE . . . . . . . . . . . . . . . 40
78. A MYSTERIOUS TRIANGLE . . . . . . . . . . . . . . . 40
79. SLICED AND FLATTENED BOX . . . . . . . . . . . . . 41
80. A SQUARE ON A SQUARE . . . . . . . . . . . . . . . . 41
81. TRIANGULAR LAND . . . . . . . . . . . . . . . . . . . 42
82. ADD THE ANGLES . . . . . . . . . . . . . . . . . . . . 42

## CHAPTER 5 – GAMES, LOGICAL TESTS AND OTHERS

83. ENIGMATIC GIRLS . . . . . . . . . . . . . . . . . . . . 44
84. A CUBE WITH HOLES IN IT . . . . . . . . . . . . . . . 44
85. DEDUCTION AT A ROUND TABLE . . . . . . . . . . . 45
86. ERASED MARKS . . . . . . . . . . . . . . . . . . . . . 46
87. THE YOUNGEST OR THE OLDEST? . . . . . . . . . . . 46
88. STRANGE VILLAGES AND A FIRE . . . . . . . . . . . 47
89. INTERROGATION . . . . . . . . . . . . . . . . . . . . 48
90. QUESTIONABLE DIVISIBILITY BY 10 . . . . . . . . . 48
91. ARRANGING MARBLES . . . . . . . . . . . . . . . . . 49
92. SUM OF 50 EQUALS 100 . . . . . . . . . . . . . . . . . 49
93. MUSHROOM PROBLEMS . . . . . . . . . . . . . . . . 50
94. COLOR BALLS . . . . . . . . . . . . . . . . . . . . . . 50
95. DECEPTIVE PRIZE . . . . . . . . . . . . . . . . . . . . 50
96. STEM UP, STEM DOWN . . . . . . . . . . . . . . . . . 51
97. WRITING IN DIGITS . . . . . . . . . . . . . . . . . . . 52
98. ADDING UP TO 100 . . . . . . . . . . . . . . . . . . . . 52
99. PLAYING MATCHES . . . . . . . . . . . . . . . . . . . 53
100. TILES ON THE TAPE . . . . . . . . . . . . . . . . . . . 53

## SOLUTIONS . . . . . . . . . . . . . . . . . . . . . . . 54

# CHAPTER 1

## NATURAL NUMBERS AND INTEGERS

## 1. AT THE BOOKSTORE

Agatha was going to buy eight books, but it turned out she was $7 short. What she did was buy just seven books and was left with $5 to spare. How much did a single book cost if all the titles she was interested in cost the same?

## 2. AQUARIUM

A cuboidal glass aquarium filled to the brim with water weighs 108 lb. The very same vessel half filled weighs 57 lb. How much does the empty aquarium weigh?

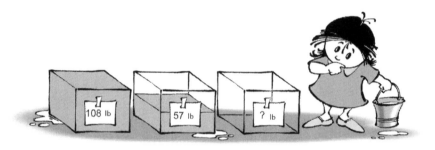

## 3. MULTIPLYING THE SPOTS

In the figure below, find the mystery domino tile which yields a correct operation of multiplication of a three-digit number by a one-digit number, and whose product equals 2532?

## 4. THE YEAR OF SOPHIE'S BIRTH

In January 1993, Sophie's age equaled the sum of digits comprised in her birth year. What year was Sophie born in?

## 5. I WILL NOT BE A TRIANGLE!

Kate has found six two-digit numbers, such that no three of them can constitute the lengths of a triangle's sides.
Can you find such numbers?
*Reminder: Given that a, b, c > 0 are the lengths of a certain triangle, if a + b > c, b + c > a, and c + a > b, then the length of any side of the triangle is smaller than the sum of the lengths of the two remaining sides.*

## 6. A MEASURE OF SUGAR

With a double pan scale and only four weights of 1-oz, 3-oz, 9-oz, and 27-oz, how does one measure 15 oz of sugar, and then 25 oz?

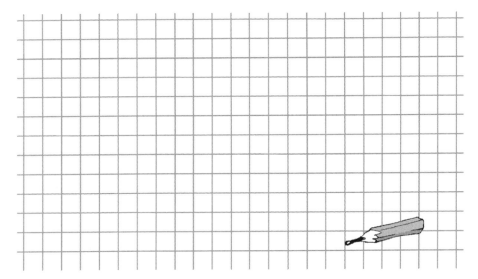

# 7. RIDDLE MAN

When Augustus de Morgan (a mathematician who was born and died in the 19th century) was asked about his age, he replied: "I was $x$ years old in the year $x^2$"
What year was he born in? Could such a strange lot have befallen someone who was born and died in the 20th century?

# 8. WHAT DID TOM WRITE?

Tom wrote down two positive integers consisting of the following digits: 1, 2, 3, 4, 5, and 6. Each of the digits appeared in only one of the two numbers, and only once. When Tom added up these numbers, he obtained 750. What positive integers did Tom write?

# 9. NINE-DIGIT NUMBERS

Out of the digits 1, 2, 3, 4, 5, 6, 7, 8, and 9, a nine-digit number was formed in which each of the digits enumerated occurred only once, and in addition, each digit was either greater by 5 or smaller by 4 than the preceding one. How many such numbers can be formed?

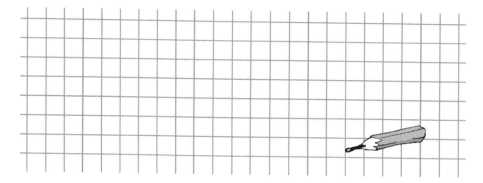

## 10. PUPILS AND GEOMETRY

The teacher gave her Class-five pupils a difficult geometry problem to solve. It turned out that the number of boys who solved it was greater by one than the number of girls who failed to do so. Which group outnumbered the other: All the pupils that solved the problem or all the girls?

## 11. WAX CLOCKS

We are given three candles, the first of which burns out in 4 minutes, the second one in 5 minutes, and the third in 9 minutes. How can we possibly measure 6 minutes by lighting and blowing out the candles? Our assumption holds that both lighting and blowing out take place instantly.

## 12. A PECULIAR NUMBER SEQUENCE

Does a sequence of 11 integers other than zero exists and whose sum of seven successive terms is always positive, whereas the sum of all its terms is a negative number?

Clue: Does an $a$, $b$, $c$ three-term sequence exist in which $a + b + c < 0$, but $a + b > 0$ and $b + c > 0$?

## 13. DOTS ON THE SIDES

Ann and Kate are sitting face to face and are looking at a big die lying between them. Each girl sees the upper side of the dice and only two of the four lateral sides, but neither sees the same lateral ones. Ann has counted 10 dots on the three sides she is facing, whereas Kate sees 14 dots on the sides in front of her. How many dots are there on the side unseen by the girls?
*Note: The sum of dots on opposite sides is always 7.*

## 14. ABSENT-MINDED JOAN

Joan was helping her aunt run a candy shop. When the shop closed after a day's work, the girl counted all the chocolate bars that remained on the shelves, but due to her absent-mindedness, the number she wrote down in her notebook was missing its final digit. The following morning, her aunt found to her surprise that the number of chocolate bars on the shelves was greater by 89 than the number found in Joan's notebook. What was the number Joan should have written down?

## 15. A MATTER OF AGE

Two sisters, Barbara and Monica, celebrate their birthday together since they were born on the same day and in the same month, except that Barbara is two years younger than Monika. To a tactless question about her age, Monica replied with a smile: "Barbara is very young – she is not as old as we were together nine years ago. As for me, I am very old, because I am older than we were together nine years ago."
How old is each sister now?

## 16. NEW YORK HAS THE UPPER HAND!

The final score of the hockey game between the New York Islanders and the Boston Bruins was 9 to 5. Is it possible that partway through the game, there must have come a moment in which the Bruins had exactly the same number of goals as the Islanders scored in the remainder of the game?

## 17. A CHOCOLATE PROBLEM

A shopkeeper has 30 chocolate bars, each of which weighs 2, 3 or 4 ounces. The total weight of the bars is 100 ounces. Which bars does the shopkeeper have more: 2 or 4-oz bars?

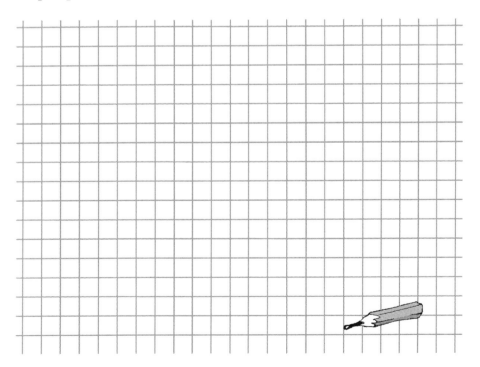

## 18. KINGLETS

A certain king has numerous offspring. His eldest son is a twin, and the remaining children – apart from seven – are also twins. In addition, all the king's children are triplets except those seven. How many children does the king have?

## 19. EVEN? ODD? EVEN?...

Integer $m$ is the square of a certain two-digit number, and it ends with 5. Is the third digit from last of this $m$ number even or odd?

## 20. GREAT CONTEST FOR AUTHORS OF MATH PROBLEMS

Ten 6th grade pupils submitted 35 interesting math problems of their own. Among the participants, there was at least one person who submitted one problem, at least one that submitted two, and at least one submitted three. The most entries have been submitted by Steve. What is the smallest possible number of problems he could have submitted?

# 21. TOM AND HIS SEQUENCES

Tom has written numbers 1, 2, 3, 4, 5, 6, and 7 in one sequence, but in such an order that if we cross out any three numbers, there will always remain four numbers, which do not form a descending nor an ascending sequence. Can you possibly recreate the sequence given by Tom? Is there but only one way of forming such a sequence?

# 22. SAYS AGATHA

Agatha says that if you write the numbers 1, 2, 3, 4, 5, and 6 in any order, you will always be able to cross out three of them in such a way that the remaining three should form a sequence either ascending or descending. Is Agatha right?

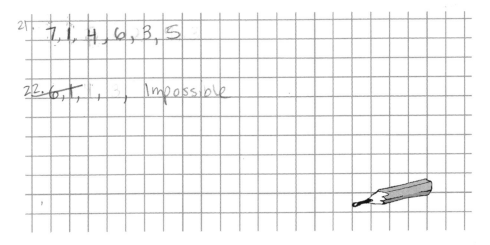

21. 7, 1, 4, 6, 3, 5

22. 6, 1, , , Impossible

## 23. ONE SESSION AFTER ANOTHER

During his five-year studies, a student passed 33 exams. Each following year, he wrote fewer exams than the previous year. The number of his first-year exams was three times greater than the number of his final-year exams. How many exams did the student have in his third year?

## 24. DIGITS 'RESHUFFLE'

Three three-digit numbers, in which are represented all digits except zero, add up to make 1,665. In each of these numbers, we reverse the first and last digit, and we add up the new numbers obtained in this way. What will their sum be?

## 25. REMEMBER YOUR PIN

To remember certain codes or passwords, such as the PIN number, it is advisable to establish relationships between the digits that make them up since it has been noticed that such relationships tend to be retained in our memory much longer than the numbers themselves. Bill noticed that in his four-digit cell phone PIN, the second digit (counting from the left) is the sum of the last two digits, and the first is the quotient of the last two. Moreover, the first two digits and the last two are made up of two two-digit numbers whose sum equals 100. Find Bill's cellular phone PIN.

# CHAPTER 2

## DIVISIBILITY AND PRIME NUMBERS

## 26. HOW OLD IS MR. WILSON?

The Wilsons were born in the 20<sup>th</sup> century. Mrs. Wilson is a year younger than her husband. The sum of the digits of the year in which the husband was born and the sum of the digits of the year in which his wife was born are integers divisible by 4. What year was Mr. Wilson born in?

## 27. MR. T'S SONS

The age of each of Mr. Triangle's three sons is an integer. The sum of these integers equals 12, and their arithmetic product is 30. How old is each of Mr. Triangle's sons?

## 28. MYSTERIOUS MULTIPLICATION

What digits should be substituted for *A* and *B* to obtain a correct equation: $AB \times A \times B = BBB$, where *AB* is a two-digit number and *BBB* is a three-digit one?

## 29. A ONE HUNDRED-HEADED DRAGON

Once upon a time, there lived a fierce dragon, which had a hundred heads. With a stroke of his sword, the knight could cut off one, seven or 11 heads, but if at least one head remained uncut, immediately after the sword stroke, there grew back four, one, or five heads, respectively. Was the knight able to kill the dragon, then? What would be the answer if the dragon had initially had 99 heads?

*Remember: The dragon dies if after the sword stroke he has no more heads.*

## 30. THE POWER OF A WEIRD NUMBER

Is it true that any power of the number 376 (with a positive integer exponent) ends with these three digits: 376?

## 31. A COLUMN OF PLASTIC TROOPS

Bart has an army of plastic soldiers. When he tried to form with his soldiers a column of fours, in the last row remained only three figures. When Bart formed a column of threes, the last row consisted of only two soldiers. How many soldiers will he have in the last row if he forms a column of sixes?

## 32. THE MAID OF ORLÉANS

Joan of Arc was burned at the stake on May 30 in the year which is a four-digit odd number divisible by 27 and which begins with the digit 1. The product of its digits is 12. What year did Joan of Arc perish in?

## 33. SPECIAL NATURAL NUMBERS

Can you find 10 different natural numbers whose sum is a number divisible by each of these numbers?
*Clue: You should start your attempt to solve this problem with three natural numbers.*

## 34. INTEGER BREAK DOWN

Can each natural number greater than 5 be represented as the sum of a prime number and a composite number?

## 35. DIVIDE NUMBERS

The sum of positive integers $a_1 + a_2 + a_3 + \ldots + a_{49}$ equals 999. What value can the greatest common divisor (GCD) of the following numbers $a_1, a_2, a_3, \ldots,$ and $a_{49}$ assume?

## 36. THE MAGNIFICENT SEVEN

Seven integers have been chosen such that the sum of any two numbers is divisible by 7. How many numbers of the selected set are divisible by 7?

# 37. NOSTRADAMUS AND HIS PROPHECY

According to Nostradamus, a famous French apothecary and a famous seer (1503-1566), exceptional are those years which written in the decimal system have the form *abcd* and comply with $ab + cd = bc$, where *ab*, *cd* and *bc* denote two-digit numbers which are also written in the decimal system. It is assumed at the same time that if $c = 0$, then $0d$ denotes a single-digit number *d*. For instance, the year 1208 was exceptional because 12 + + 08 = 20. Which nearest year after 2006 will be exceptional?

# 38. SQUARE RIDDLE

Does a natural number denoted by *a* exist such that $(a^2 + 2006)$ is the square of a natural number?

## 39. MULTIPLY AND ADD, MULTIPLY AND ADD…

A natural number was multiplied by 2, and the obtained product was increased by 1. Then, the obtained number was multiplied again by 2, and 1 was also added to the result.

The above two-step operation was repeated five times. Can the final result be a number:

a) Divisible by 7?

b) Divisible by 12?

## 40. PLAY ON NUMBERS

On the blackboard were numbers: 1, 2, 3, …, 110. In each move, you were supposed to cross out any two numbers and replace them with their difference. After 109 moves, there remained on the blackboard but one number. Could it be number 10?

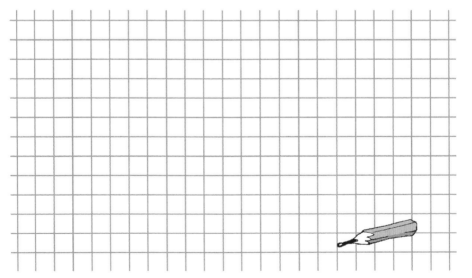

22

# CHAPTER 3

## EQUATIONS

## 41. ZERO-SUM GAME

Tom and Simon were casting in turns a single die when they thought of such a game: If a one is thrown by either player, Tom pays Simon 50 cents, but when some other value comes out, Simon pays Tom 10 cents. After 30 throws, it turned out that they were square, and neither of them won 'a penny'. How many times did a one come out?

## 42. THE CHINESE AND THEIR BICYCLES

In a certain Chinese village live 29 families. Each family has one, two or three bicycles. There are as many families owning three bicycles as families with only one. How many bicycles are there in the village?

## 43. LONG JUMP COMPETITION

In a school long jump competition, Mark came seventh, whereas his friend David was sixth. William, however, did better than his two friends and averaged out, which means that he lost to the same number of jumpers as he beat. Paul jumped worse than Mark and finally came in the penultimate position. How many boys took part in the competition?

## 44. CALLING A SPADE A SPADE IN THE GARDEN

A father and his son take 8 hours to dig the entire plot of land. The father working by himself needs 12 hours to accomplish the task. How many hours will it take the son to dig the plot by himself?

## 45. FAST CREEPERS

Two snails, Daniel and Sebastian, are racing against each other along a track divided into three sections. Each section measures exactly one meter. Daniel creeps at a constant speed, whereas Sebastian covers the first section of the racetrack at a speed twice as high as Daniel, the second section at the same speed as Daniel, and the third one at half the speed of his rival. Who is going to win, and by how many meters?

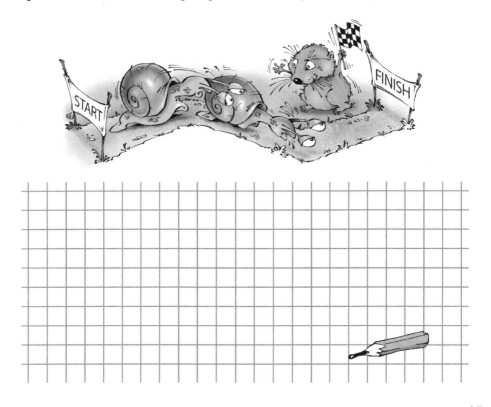

## 46. CAKE LOVERS

At the cake shop, there are three
types of cakes – their prices are
in round dollars. For a dollar,
you can get a cream cake, two
fruit cakes, or three doughnuts.
Two brothers, Jeremy and Roger,

had been given $11 by their parents and invited a group of backyard
kids to have cakes together. The group consisted of as many boys as
girls. Each kid was treated to the same set of cakes, which consisted of
the same number of the same cakes. How big was the group of kids?

## 47. CHIP IN FOR A NEW BALL

Three boys have bought a football for $45.
The first boy gave an amount that did not
exceed what the remaining two boys chipped
in. The second boy added no more than half
of the sum paid by the first and third boy
together. The third boy, however, chipped
in no more than a fifth of the amount
contributed by the two remaining boys. How
much did each boy pay for the ball?

## 48. PRACTICAL JOKERS

Will and Ken love playing tricks on one another.
Yesterday they were going down on the escalator
in the shopping mall. When the boys were half
way down, Will snatched Ken's baseball cap
off the top of his head and threw it onto
the escalator travelling in the opposite
direction. Ken in no time shot up
for the top of the escalator
to regain his cap. Will, on
the other hand, ran first
downstairs and then up the

escalator to catch Ken's cap still faster. The boys ran at the same speed, no matter whether downward or upward (their speed was twice as high as that of the escalator). Who reached the baseball cap first?

## 49. HEAD START FOR DAVE

Andrew is a far better runner than Dave, and in a 100 meter race, he breaks the finish line tape when Dave has still 20 meters to go. Their friend Joe drew an additional line 20 meters before the actual starting line and said: "Let Dave begin at the official starting line and Andrew at the new one. If they start at the same time and run at their usual speeds, they will finish the race neck and neck."
Is Joe right? If not, what distance from the starting line should the new one be drawn in order that both runners reach the finishing line simultaneously?

# 50. QUARRELS ALONG THE WAY

During a school trip attended by all Class 5B pupils, there arose several misunderstandings, which resulted in the class dividing into two separate groups. If Sophie decided to leave group 1 and join group 2,  the first one would number $\frac{1}{3}$ of the class. If, however, Adam, Michael and Will left the second group for the first, the latter would make up half of the class. How many pupils attend Class 5B?

# 51. A HARD NUT TO CRACK

Imagine 2005 fractions:

$$\frac{2}{2006}, \frac{3}{2005}, \frac{4}{2004}, ..., \frac{2004}{4}, \frac{2005}{3}, \frac{2006}{2}.$$

Can you choose three fractions out of them, whose product will equal 1?

# 52. THE SMALLEST NUMBER OUT OF THREE

Which of the following numbers is the smallest:

$$\frac{124}{421}, \frac{124124}{421421}, \frac{1240124}{4210421}?$$

# 53. SUM UP IN THE SIMPLEST WAY

Give a simple way to calculate the sum:

$$\frac{1}{10\times11} + \frac{1}{11\times12} + ... + \frac{1}{19\times20}.$$

## 54. WATERMELON HALVES

Catherine sold watermelons in the market.

The first customer, Ms. Angela, bought half the watermelons there were and a half of one. The second customer, Ms. Barbara, bought half of the remaining fruit and the very half Ms. Angela had left behind. The third customer, Ms. Cindy, again bought half of what remained and a half of one fruit. As there were no takers for the last watermelon, Catherine brought it home. What were her day's takings if she sold the fruit at 2 dollars apiece?

## 55. BUNNIES FOR SALE

A certain rabbit keeper brought his rabbits to the market. The first customer bought $\frac{1}{6}$ of all the animals plus 1; the second buyer again took $\frac{1}{6}$ of the remaining rabbits + 2; the third customer bought $\frac{1}{6}$ of the remaining animals + 3, and so on. When the man had sold all his rabbits, he found to his surprise that each customer had bought the same number of rabbits. How many rabbits did the salesman bring to the market, and how many customers did he have?

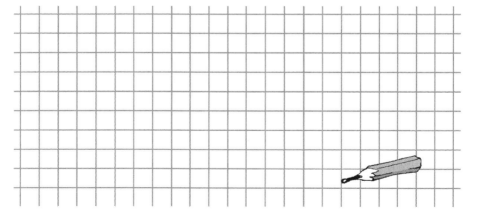

## 56. VORACIOUS SHEEP

The flock numbers eight sheep. The first sheep gobbles up a sheaf of hay in one day; the second one takes two days to eat up such a portion; the third sheep needs three days, and the fourth four days, etc. The sheaves are identical. Which sheep will devour their hay faster: the first two or the remaining six?

## 57. MICHAEL THE PROFLIGATE

Michael went to the market. A quarter of an hour later, he met Matthew, a friend of his, and said: "I have already spent half the money I had on me when I came here. As it is, I am left with as much in cents as I had in dollars, but half as much in dollars as I had in cents." Michael's riddle got Matthew thinking. He started to wonder what sum of money Michael had brought to the market. Help him find out.

## 58. THE TWINS AND THE REST

Jack is four years older than Mark and eight years older than Dave. The product from Mark's and Paul's ages is greater by 16 than the product from Jack's and Dave's ages. In this foursome, two boys are twins. Give their names.

## 59. THE CASHIER'S MISTAKE

Michael went to his bank to cash a check. The cashier, quite by mistake, paid him out as much in dollars as he should have had paid in cents, and as much in cents as he should have had paid in dollars. Michael did not count the money before pocketing it and paid no attention to a five-cent coin that he dropped on the floor in the process. He counted the money at home and found to his surprise that he had twice as much as the amount on the check. How much did Michael's check amount to?

## 60. CLASS IN PAIRS

When Class 5A pupils stood in pairs in the school courtyard, it turned out that the number of mixed pairs (a boy and girl) is equal to the remaining pairs. How many pupils does Class 5A number, given that there are 14 boys, and that the girls are the minority?

## 61. ANNA'S AGE

Maria is 24 years old. It is twice as many years as Anna had when Maria was as old as Anna is now. How old is Anna?

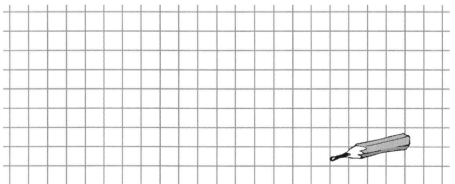

# 62. HOW OLD IS GRANNY?

# 63. MUSHROOM GATHERING

Joe and Alex picked three times as many mushrooms as Frank, while Alex and Frank had five times more mushrooms than Joe. Who collected more mushrooms: Joe with Frank or Alex alone?

# 64. GAMBLERS

Ben was talking his friend Len into a game of Battleship: "Anytime we play, the stake will be half the money there is in your pocket at the moment. How much do you have now?"

"32 bucks," answered Len.

"If you win, you will pocket an additional $16. If you happen to lose, you will give $16 to me. But don't you worry: We will play a few games, and it so happens that you win more often."

Having established the rules, the boys played seven games. Len won four times and Ben only three times. How much money does Len have now?

*Note: We don't know the exact sequence of Len's wins and losses.*

# 65. AM I THE POWER?

In a decimal representation of a certain natural number, each digit, i.e., 1, 2, 3, 4, 5, 6, 7, 8, 9, and 0, occurs the same number of times. Could this number be a power of 2?

# 66. A USED UP WHEEL

Michael and Matthew chipped in to buy a grinding wheel (22 inches in diameter) with a $3\frac{1}{7}$ inch mounting hole in the middle. Since they live 10 miles apart, they agreed that Matthew would be the first to take it, and when half of it would be used up, he would give it to Michael. What diameter will the wheel have when it changes hands? *Clue: The circle's area is expressed as $\pi R^2$, where R is the length of the radius.*

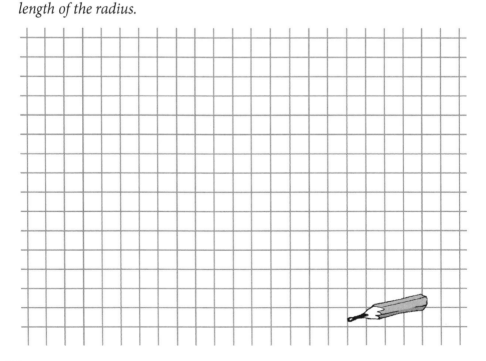

# CHAPTER 4

## GEOMETRY

# 67. ROADSIDE VILLAGES

Alongside a road, there are five villages. Let's call them *A*, *B*, *C*, *D*, and *E*, for short. The distance from *A* to *D* is known to be 6 miles, from *A* to *E* – 16 miles, from *D* to *E* – 22 miles, from *D* to *C* – 6 miles, and from *A* to *B* – 16 miles. The distances were measured along the road. Find the right order in which the villages are located along the road.

# 68. DIVIDE THE TRAPEZOID INTO TWO

How can you divide the trapezoid into two parts so that after being folded, they will form a triangle?

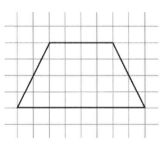

# 69. DIVIDE THE TRAPEZOID INTO FOUR

Divide the trapezoid presented below into four identical (i.e., adjacent) parts.

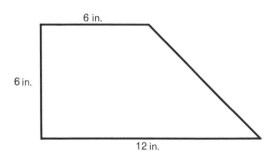

6 in.

6 in.

12 in.

## 70. CUTTING THE FIGURE INTO THREE

A plane figure consists of two squares such that $AB = BC$ (see figure). Divide the figure with two perpendicular cuttings so that after translation of the three parts, they form one square.

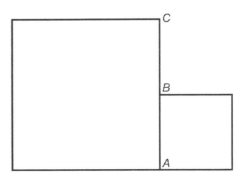

## 71. RECTANGLE OF SQUARES

The rectangle presented in the figure below consists of six squares, the smallest of them having two-inch sides. Can you calculate the area of the rectangle?
*Note: The figure is not to scale!*

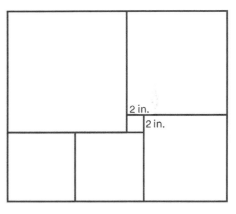

2 in.
2 in.

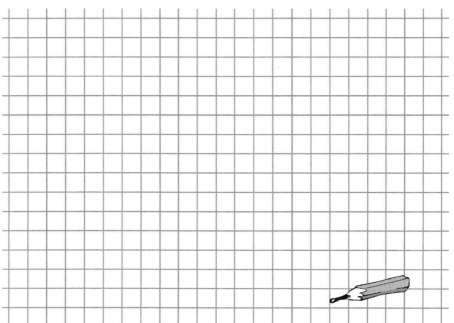

## 72. A BIT OF WHITE, A BIT OF GREEN

A rectangular, white sheet of paper with vertices *ABCD* and an area of 20 in² was folded and pressed in such a way that its opposite vertices *A* and *C* touched each other. In this way, pentagon *BCD'EF* was created with an area of 12 in²; both sides were painted green, and then unfolded to regain the initial rectangle. One side of the rectangle is now two-color. What is the area of its white side?

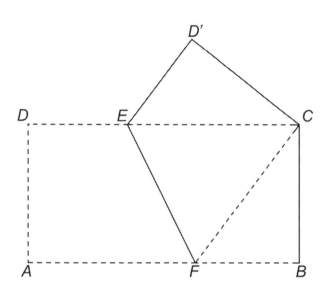

## 73. THE CUTTING STRAIGHT LINE

A straight line cut a square in such a way that it divided the square's perimeter in a ratio of 9:7, and two sides of the square in a ratio 7:1 and 5:3. In what ratio did the straight line divide the square's area?

## 74. CIRCUMFERENCES OF THE FOUR

Four identical circles intersect in such a way that the length of each shorter arc equals 3 in. What is the circumference of each circle?

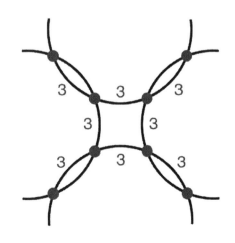

# 75. TRIANGLE NOT SO STRAIGHT

The figure below depicts half a circle with radius $R = 10$ in. Points $B$ and $C$ divide the semicircle $AD$ into three equal arcs. Calculate the shaded area of the curvilinear triangle $ABC$.

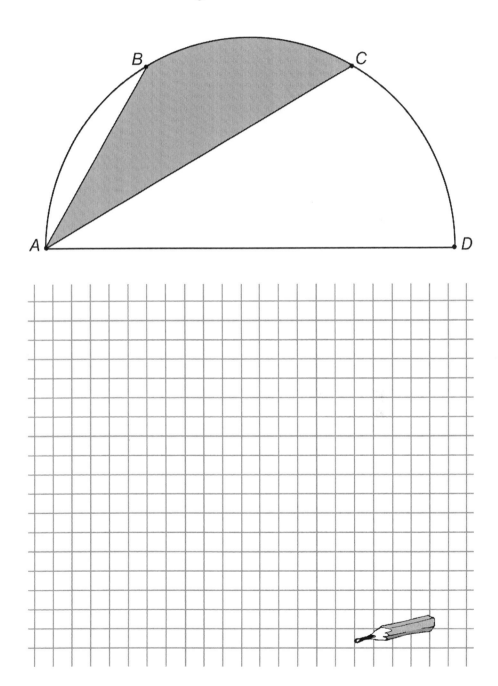

## 76. A CLEVER SISTER

Nicholas marked points *P* and *Q* on the sides of square *ABCD* in such places that the sum of the lengths of the segments *PB* and *BQ* was equal to the length of the side of square *ABCD*. Then, he used a protractor to measure three angles: *PAQ*, *PCQ*, *PDQ* at which segment *PQ* is observed from vertices *A*, *C*, and *D* of square *ABCD*. As the next step, Nicholas added the magnitudes of these angles and was very surprised to obtain a round sum. His elder sister Ann cast an eye over the figure, and making no measurements, calculated in her head the sum of magnitudes of the angles. How did she do it?

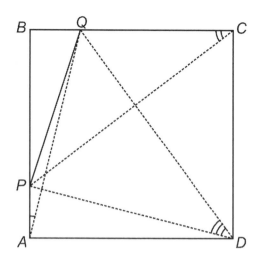

## 77. CIRCLES ON A TRIANGLE

The perimeter of a triangle with vertices *D*, *E* and *F* equals 30 in. The centers of circles $C_D$, $C_E$ and $C_F$ coincide with the marked vertices of the triangle, that is in points *D*, *E*, and *F*. Circles $C_D$ and $C_E$ are externally tangent, and each of them is internally tangent to circle $C_F$. What is the length of the radius of circle $C_F$?

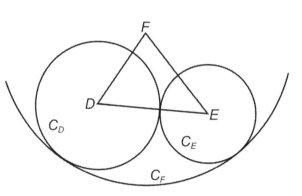

## 78. A MYSTERIOUS TRIANGLE

In a certain triangle, each angle is smaller than the sum of the two remaining angles. What can we say about this triangle?

## 79. SLICED AND FLATTENED BOX

With a sharp knife, we cut the cardboard tetrahedron along three edges that meet at the same vertex. Then, we flatten out the cardboard and put the obtained plane figure on the table. Could the obtained figure be a square?

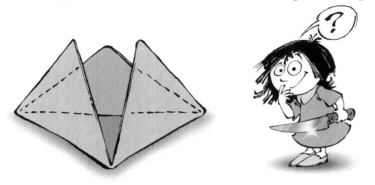

## 80. A SQUARE ON A SQUARE

The 10 in. × 10 in. *PQRS* square overlaps square *ABCD* of the same side lengths. As it turns out, the centre of square *PQRS* coincides with the vertex of square *ABCD*. Calculate the overlapping shaded area.

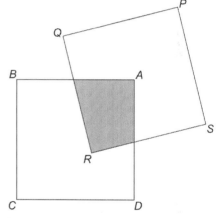

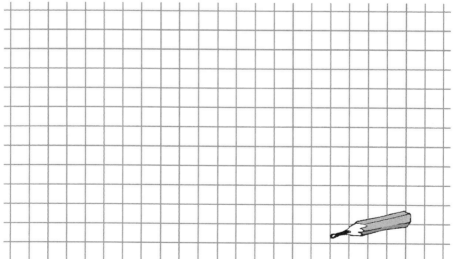

## 81. TRIANGULAR LAND

An island has the shape of a triangle. Which point lies farthest from the sea?

## 82. ADD THE ANGLES

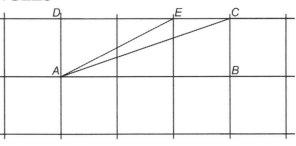

Two segments, *AC* and *AE*, have been drawn on a gridded sheet of paper. Calculate the sum of angle *BAC* and angle *BAE*.

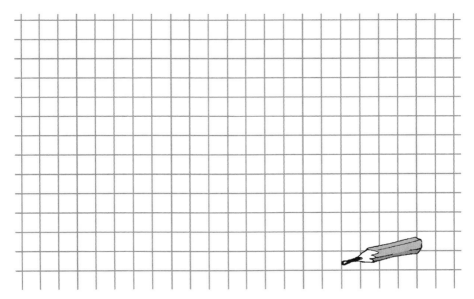

# CHAPTER 5

## GAMES, LOGICAL TESTS AND OTHERS

## 83. ENIGMATIC GIRLS

Among four girls, there are no three of the same first name, the same family name, and the same color of hair. In each pair, however, the girls have either a common first name, or a common family name, or hair of the same color. Is it possible?

## 84. A CUBE WITH HOLES IN IT

Several tiny cubes were glued together to form a 5×5×5 hexahedron in such a way that three hollow tunnels were created running across the whole solid. Their cross-sections were blackened in the figure below. Then, another such hexahedron was formed in the same way, also with hollow tunnels, but of a different shape. How many small cubes were used to build each of these hexahedrons with holes in them?

**a)**

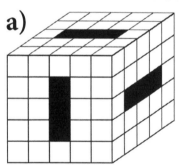

**b)**

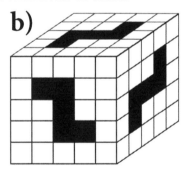

And how many cubes form the hollow hexahedrons presented in the pictures below?

**c)**

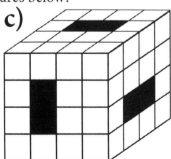

**d)**

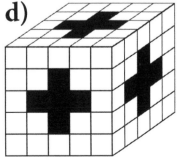

# 85. DEDUCTION AT A ROUND TABLE

Four married couples: Agatha and John, Barbara and Kevin, Celine and Leon, and Daphne and Matthew (the hosts) were celebrating Matthew's birthday. Everybody was sitting at a round table in such a way that each lady was seated between two gentlemen, and all the couples were separated. Agatha took her seat between Kevin and Matthew. Matthew sat to the right of Agatha. John was sitting next to Daphne. Who took the seat to the right of Barbara?

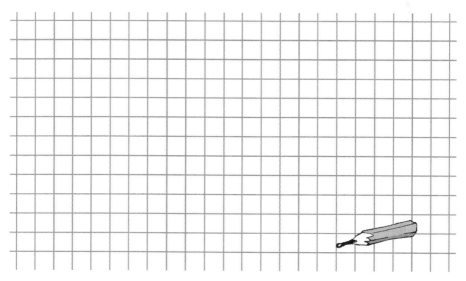

## 86. ERASED MARKS

If we erase 3 marks from an ordinary 6-in long ruler, and remove 3 numbers written below them (as in the figure below), we will get a new ruler consisting of four marks. Using this ruler, we will also be able to measure in integers each distance from 1 to 6 in. For example, we can measure 2 in., because such is the distance between the remaining marks 4 and 6.

What maximum number of marks and numbers can we remove from an 11-in ruler, and yet be able to measure each distance from 1inch up to 11?

Draw such a ruler.

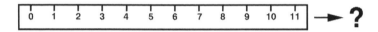

## 87. THE YOUNGEST OR THE OLDEST?

Annie, Betsy, Celine and Dorothy are four friends differing in their ages; when asked which of them was youngest, they gave the following answers:

Given that one of the girls was not telling the truth, guess which of them is the youngest and which one is the eldest.

# 88. STRANGE VILLAGES AND A FIRE

Somewhere off the beaten track lie three villages, Aden, Baden, and Caden, which share a fire brigade located outside these places. The inhabitants of Aden always tell the truth, while the locals in Baden begin their conversation with a true statement, which is invariably followed by a pack of lies. The villagers in Caden embark on their conversation with a true sentence and then alternately lie and tell the truth. One day the duty officer in the fire station received a call from an inhabitant of one of the villages:

"A fire has broken out in one of the villages!"

"In which village?" demanded the officer.

"In ours!"

"Ours?… and more precisely."

"In Caden!"

At that moment, the line went dead. Which village was the call from? And where should have the duty officer sent the fire engine?

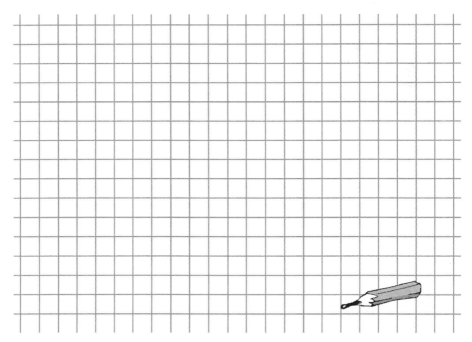

# 89. INTERROGATION

The police have arrested 6 criminals and are trying to establish which of them is the gang boss. The inspector carrying out the investigation made the suspects stand in front of him in a line-up (in the same order as in the table) and asked each of them four questions. Both the questions and answers are set out in the table below:

| No. | Questions | John | Julian | Igor | David | Peter | James |
|-----|-----------|------|--------|------|-------|-------|-------|
| 1 | Are you the gang boss? | NO | NO | NO | NO | NO | YES |
| 2 | Is the boss standing to your left? | NO | YES | NO | NO | YES | NO |
| 3 | Is the boss standing to your right? | NO | YES | YES | NO | YES | NO |
| 4 | Is the boss standing next to you? | YES | YES | YES | YES | NO | NO |

Each criminal lied exactly twice. Can you, on the basis of the above answers, identify the gang boss?
*Note: To the left of Igor stands David, and to his right, Julian.*

# 90. QUESTIONABLE DIVISIBILITY BY 10

We have 6 positive integers. Is it true that among them there must be two such numbers whose sum or difference is divisible by 10?

# 91. ARRANGING MARBLES

Anne has three boxes marked (W, W), (G, G) and (W, G) and six marbles, which she arranged in pairs in such a way that the first pair consists of two white marbles, the second of two green, and the third of one green and one white marble. The girl is going to put each pair of marbles into one of the boxes so that the letters on the box will correspond with its contents. However, due to a careless mistake of hers, all the pairs of marbles found themselves put in the wrong boxes. Now we are supposed to take out only one marble from one of the boxes without seeing the remaining marbles. On the basis of the color of the marble we have just taken out, we must determine which box contains the pair of white marbles and which box contains the pair of green marbles. How can we do that?

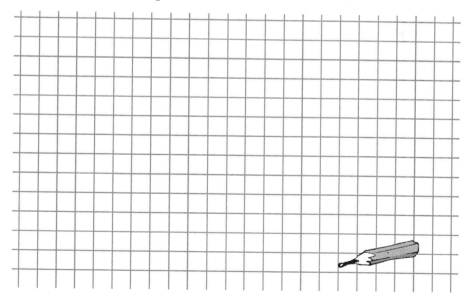

# 92. SUM OF 50 EQUALS 100

The sum of fifty numbers $a_1 + a_2 + a_3 + \ldots a_{50}$ equals 100.
The question is whether among these 50 numbers there must be three numbers whose sum equals at least 6.

## 93. MUSHROOM PROBLEMS

There are 30 mushrooms in a basket. If we choose at random 12 mushrooms, there will be at least one cep among them, and if we choose 20 mushrooms, we will pick at least one brown ring boletus. How many ceps are there in the basket?

## 94. COLOR BALLS

In a box, there are 30 one-color balls of three different colors. If we randomly take 25 balls out of the box, among our picks will always be at least three white, at least five blue, and at least seven black balls. How many balls of each color are there in the box?

## 95. DECEPTIVE PRIZE

Mark marked six points on a sheet of paper as shown in the picture below, and he said to Sophie:
"Get two crayons: A red one and a blue one." Connect each pair of points with a line segment, using either red or blue color in such a way as not to get a one-color triangle. If you perform the task successfully, I will give you a chocolate bar.
Has Sophie been given the prize?

# 96. STEM UP, STEM DOWN

Five wineglasses have been arranged in a row as shown in the picture below and numbered from 1 to 5.

Two players take part in the game, and they make moves in turns. However, only two kinds of moves are allowed:

1) Any wineglass standing stem side up can be placed the other way round, i.e., stem side down.

2) You can turn two wineglasses standing side by side if the one standing on the right is upside down.

The winner is the player after whose move all the glasses will be standing on their stems. Does the player beginning the game have a winning strategy (i.e., he can always win, irrespective of what his opponent does)?

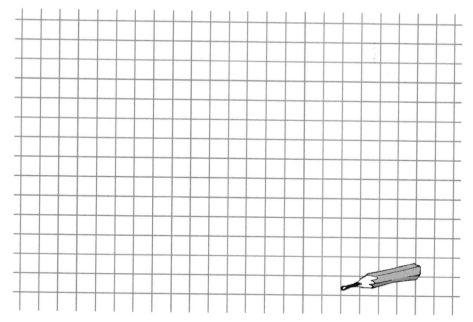

## 97. WRITING IN DIGITS

In the next game, two players alternately write one of the digits of a 12-digit number. If the formed 12-digit number is divisible by 3, the winner is the player who started the game; otherwise, the second one wins. The following rules hold:

a) The first digit cannot equal zero.
b) Digits different from 9 can only be followed by a greater digit.
c) Digit 9 can be followed by any digit.

Which of the players has the winning strategy?
*Reminder: You should bear in mind that a number is divisible by 3 if and only if the sum of the digits of this number is divisible by 3.*

## 98. ADDING UP TO 100

Adam and Bill decided to have a game of adding up to 100. It is Adam who begins. His first step is to write down a natural number no greater than 10; then it is Bill's turn, who increases the number by no more than 10, but by no less than 1. Likewise, Adam increases the newly formed number by no more than 10, but by at least 1. The two players make such alternate moves until the player who first reaches 100 is pronounced the winner. Does the beginning player have a winning strategy? If so, what first move should he make, and what will be his responses to the numbers written down by his opponent?

## 99. PLAYING MATCHES

There are 48 matchsticks in
the box. Players make moves
alternately. Each player can take
out one, two, or five matchsticks
from the box (if it is not empty).
The winner is the person who
takes out the last matchsticks, leaving his opponent with an empty box.
Does the player beginning the game have the winning strategy? If so,
what move should he make first? What would be the answer if the box
initially contained 49 matchsticks?

## 100. TILES ON THE TAPE

Mark and Daniel are alternately laying down domino tiles on a tape
divided into 13 squares. Each tile covers exactly two squares. A tile can
be placed on two empty squares; you cannot possibly put one tile on top
of another. The winner is the player who covers the last empty square
(after his move, there are no two free adjacent squares). It is Mark who
begins; as the starting player, can he win the game? What would be the
answer if the tape consisted of 14 squares?

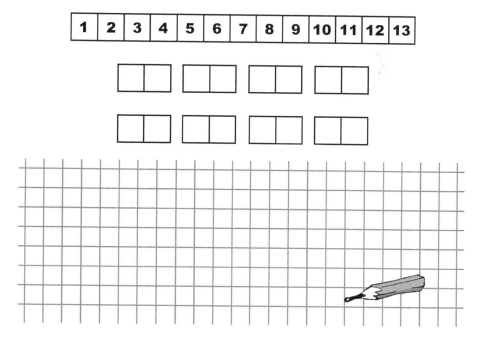

# SOLUTIONS

## CHAPTER 1

### NATURAL NUMBERS AND INTEGERS

**1.** Having bought seven books, Agatha was left with $5. To buy the eighth book, she needed an extra $7. That is why we know that the book cost $5 + $7 = $12, just like each one she actually bought.
**Answer: Each book costs $12.**

**2.** The difference between the aquarium filled to capacity and half empty is 108 – 57 = 51 lb – this is the weight of the water in the half-filled aquarium. The empty container weighs as much as the half filled aquarium (57 lb) minus the water weight, i.e., 57 – 51 = 6.
**Answer: The empty aquarium weighs 6 lb.**

**3.** The second factor in the multiplication must be number 4. If it was 3 or a smaller number, then the product would equal at most 639 × 3 < 2000. If, however, the second factor was 5 or a greater number, then the product would equal at least 630 × 5 > 3000. In that case, the first factor is equal to 2532 ÷ 4 = 633.
**Answer: The missing domino tile is the 3-4 tile (three spots at the top and four spots at the bottom).**

**4.** The sum of digits of the year earlier than 1993 equals no more than 1 + 9 + 9 + 9 = 28, so Sophie is 28 years old at most. This means that Sophie was born in 1993 – 28 = 1965, at the earliest. The sum of digits of any year between 1965 and 1993 equals at least 1 + 9 + 6 + 0 = 16, thus Sophie was born at the latest in 1993 – 16 = 1977. Let us consider two cases:

a) Sophie was born in the sixties, i.e., in the year 1960 + $x$, where $x$ is a single-digit number. The sum of the digits of the year in which she was born equals $1 + 9 + 6 + x = 16 + x$. Sophie would be $16 + x$ years old in the year $1960 + x + 16 + x = 1976 + 2x$, i.e., this year is expressed by an even number. However, it transpires from the riddle that Sophie would be $16 + x$ years in the year 1993, which is an odd number. In that case, Sophie can't have been born in the sixties.

b) Sophie was born in the seventies, i.e., in the year 1970 + $x$, where $x$ is a single-digit number. The sum of the digits of the year she was born in is $1 + 9 + 7 + x = 17 + x$. Thus Sophie would be $17 + x$ years old in the year $1970 + x + 17 + x = 1987 + 2x = 1993$, hence $2x = 1993 - 1987 = 6$; $x = 3$, so the year to find is 1973.

**Answer: Sophie was born in 1973.**


**5.** Let's start with two smallest possible 2-digit numbers, i.e., 10 and 10. Since $a + 10 > 10$ for $a > 0$, so in order for 10, 10 and $a$ not to be side lengths of any triangle, we should assume that $a$ is meeting the condition $a \geq 10 + 10 = 20$.

Let's again assume the smallest possible number, i.e., 20.

Considering further: if $b > 0$ and $b < 20$, then 10, 10 and $b$ are side lengths of a certain triangle; similarly, if $b > 10$, and $b < 30$, then 10, 20 and $b$ are side lengths of a certain triangle. As the fourth number, we can then assume the sum of the two greatest numbers out of the ones chosen so far, i.e., $10 + 20 = 30$, etc. In this way we will obtain six numbers: 10, 10, 20, 30, 50, and 80, of which no three can be side lengths of a triangle.

**Answer: A set of numbers satisfying the conditions presented above are for example: 10, 10, 20, 30, 50, and 80 (also 11, 12, 24, 37, 62, and 99; etc.).**


**6.** On one pan of the scale, we put the 27-oz weight. On the other, we put the 3 and 9-oz weights and add sugar until the pans have reached equilibrium.

On the scale, we will have $27 - 3 - 9 = 15$ ounces of sugar.

To weigh out 25 ounces of sugar, it is enough to put a 27-oz weight with a 1-oz weight on one pan, and a 3-oz weight on the second, and add sugar till the pans are at equilibrium. The weight of sugar will be $27 + 1 - 3 = 25$ ounces.

**7.** The year $x^2$ must have been in the 19th century. We check and see that the only square in the range of 1801 to 1900 is the number $43^2 = 1849$. De Morgan was thus 43 years old in the year $43^2 = 1849$, hence he was born in 1849 – 43 = 1806.

As for the second part of the problem: Let us assume that someone was $y$ years old in the year $y^2$ in the 20th century. The only square in the range from 1901 to 2000 is $44^2 = 1936$. If this was the case, the person in question would have been 44 years old in the year 1936, and he thus must have been born in the year 1936 – 44 = 1892. That would mean, however, that the person was born in the 19th century.

*Note: The 19th century began on January 1, 1801 and ended on December 31, 1900. The 20th century began on January 1, 1901 and ended on December 31, 2000.*

**Answer: Augustus de Morgan was born in 1806. A similar concurrence for someone living in the 20th century would have been impossible.**

**8.** Please note that both numbers must have been at most three-digit ones – otherwise their sum would have had at least four digits. We assume that these numbers are $abc$ and $def$. The sum of $c + f$ must be a number whose last digit is 0, which occurs only for $c = 4$ and $f = 6$, or $c = 6$ and $f = 4$. Since $abc + def = 750$, and $c + f = 10$, then $ab + de = 74$. Therefore, $b + e$ equals 4 or 14, hence $b = 1$ and $e = 3$, or $b = 3$ and $e = 1$. This means that $a = 2$ and $d = 5$, or $a = 5$ and $d = 2$ (only these two digits have remained).

**Answer: The possible pairs of numbers written down by Tom are: 214 and 536, 216 and 534, 234 and 516, or 236 and 514.**

**9.** The digit 1 can only be followed by the digit 6 – let us write it down as $1 \to 6$.

The digit 6 can only be followed by 2, which will be put down as $1 \to 6 \to 2$.

Proceeding further in this way we will obtain the diagram:

$$1 \to 6 \to 2 \to 7 \to 3$$
$$\uparrow \qquad\qquad\qquad\qquad \downarrow$$
$$5 \leftarrow 9 \leftarrow 4 \leftarrow 8$$

Each nine-digit number referred to in the problem can be formed if we choose the first digit (from 1 to 9), and the consecutive ones can be found in the above figure as we move in the direction of the arrows. For example, if we choose 3 as the first digit, we will obtain the number 384,951,627; on the other hand, if the first digit is 4, we will get 495,162,738. From this it transpires that there are as many such nine-digit numbers as there are possible choices of the first digit, i.e., nine. **Answer: There are nine nine-digit numbers meeting the specified conditions.**

**10.** We know from the problem that:
(the number of schoolchildren who solved the problem) = (the number of girls who solved the problem) + (the number of boys who solved the problem) = (the number of girls who solved the problem) + (the number of girls who did not solve the problem) + 1 = (the number of girls) + 1. Thus the number of schoolchildren who have solved the problem is greater by one than the number of girls in the class.
**Answer: There are more schoolchildren who have solved the problem than all the girls in the class.**

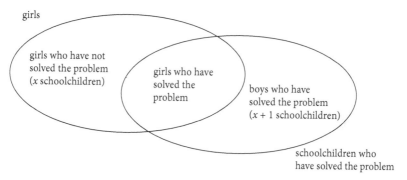

**11.** The modus operandi in consecutive minutes is presented in the table below:

| Minutes | 0 | 1 | 2 | 3 | 4 | 5 | 6 | 7 | 8 | 9 | 10 |
|---|---|---|---|---|---|---|---|---|---|---|---|
| 4-minute candle | 🕯 | 🕯 | 🕯 | 🕯 | goes out | | | | | | |
| 5-minute candle | 🕯 | 🕯 | 🕯 | 🕯 | is put out | | | | | is lit again | goes out |
| 9-minute candle | 🕯 | 🕯 | 🕯 | 🕯 | 🕯 | 🕯 | 🕯 | 🕯 | 🕯 | goes out | |
| | | | | | we begin to measure time | | | | | | 6 minutes measured out |

57

*Moment 0.* We light all three candles simultaneously.

*After 4 minutes.* The 4-minute candle goes out, and we put out the 5-minute candle (the remainder will later on let us measure out one minute) and begin to measure time.

*After 9 minutes.* The 9-minute candle burns out. This also means that 5 minutes have passed since the moment we started to measure time. To measure out 6 minutes, it is now enough to light the remainder of the 5-minute candle.

*After 10 minutes.* The remainder of the 5-minute candle has just gone out – 6 minutes have passed since we started measuring out time.

**12.** Let us consider a three-term sequence: $a$, $b$, $c$. If $a + b > 0$, but $a + b + c < 0$, then the number $c$ must be negative; similarly, $a < 0$. Since $a + b + c > 0$, then $b > 0$. This allows us to come up with an exemplary sequence, e.g., –2, 3, –2.

This simpler version lets us guess that the solution should be searched for among sequences with negative numbers at its ends and positive in between. Such conditions are satisfied by, for example, this sequence: –1, –1, –1, 1, 1, 1, 1, 1, –1, –1, –1.

**Answer: Such a sequence exists.**

**13.** The sum of all dots on the die is: $1 + 2 + 3 + 4 + 5 + 6 = 21$.
If Kate saw the hidden side instead of the upper side (while seeing the same lateral sides she sees now), then each side would be observed by no more than one girl – the girls would then see 21 dots altogether, and Kate would have $21 - 10 = 11$ dots in her field of view. However, Kate is actually looking at as many as 14 dots instead of 11. Hence the conclusion is that on the upper side there are $14 - 11 = 3$ dots more than on the lower side. Since the numbers of dots on pairs of the opposite sides are 1 and 6 (the difference in the number of dots = 5), 2 and 5 (the difference in the number of dots = 3) or 3 and 4 (the difference in the number of dots = 1), this means that on the upper side are five dots, on the lower (hidden) – two dots.

**Answer: On the hidden side of the die are 2 dots.**

**14.** If, at the end of a positive integer, we put the digit 0, this integer will increase ten times. Thus, if we put any digit at the end of such an integer, this number will increase at least 10 times. Joan could not have written in her notebook the number 10 or greater, because then the real number of chocolate bars would have been at least 10 times greater than that written by Joan, i.e., greater by at least nine times the number put down in the notebook. In that case the actual number of chocolate bars would have been greater than the number Joan put down by at least $10 \times 9 = 90$. Therefore, Joan wrote down a single-digit number $a$. The true number of chocolate bars was equal to the two-digit number $ab = 10a + b$ and was greater by 89 than that written down by Joan, that is $10a + b = a + 89$. The number $(a + 89)$ can in decimal representation begin with the digit 8 or 9, hence $a = 8$ or $a = 9$. In the first case, we get $80 + b = 97$, which is impossible, whereas in the second case, $90 + b = 98$, so $b = 8$. Joan wrote down the number 9, and in fact there were $89 + 9 = 98$ chocolate bars.

**Answer: Joan should have written down the number 98.**

**15.** Let's mark by $m$ the present age of Monica and by $b$ that of Barbara.

We have then $b + 2 = m$ and $b < (m - 9) + (b - 9) < m = b + 2$.

Hence $(m - 9) + (b - 9) = b + 1$, thus $m = 19$, while $b = m - 2 = 17$.

**Answer: Monica is 19 years old and Barbara is 17.**

**16.** We ask in this problem, whether at some point in the game the score was $n{:}b$, where $b = 9 - n$, or otherwise expressed: $b + n = 9$. This means that the moment in question was the point in the game where both teams had already scored 9 goals in total. Such a situation did take place during the game, because by the end of it, both teams had scored $9 + 5 = 14$ goals altogether, and thus one of the following score must have occurred at one point: 9:0, 8:1, 7:2, 6:3, 5:4, or 4:5.

**Answer: The moment in question did occur during the game.**

**17.** Let $a$ denote the number of 2-oz chocolate bars, and $b$ denote the number of those weighing 4 ounces. Then the number of 3-oz bars is $(30 - a - b)$, i.e., the total weight of all the bars is $2a + 4b + 3(30 - a - b) = 100$. After transformations, we get $b - a = 10$. Hence $b = a + 10$, i.e., there are more 4-oz chocolate bars than those weighing 2 ounces.

**Answer: There are more 4-oz bars.**

**18.** We represent by $x$ the number of twins pairs and by $y$ the number of threes of triplets. The number of all the king's offspring equals then $7 + 2x = 7 + 3y$, hence $2x = 3y$. Moreover, $2x \leq 7$ (apart from seven children, all are triplets, i.e., they are not twins) and $2x \geq 2$; since we know that the eldest son is a twin, the king has at least one pair of twins. It follows from equation $2x = 3y$ that $2x$ is divisible by 3. The only even number divisible by 3 that satisfies the above conditions is 6, thus $2x = 6$. The number of children is then $7 + 2x = 7 + 6 = 13$, within which number are three sets of twins and two sets of triplets: $a - a$; $b - b$; $c - c$; $d - d - d$; $e - e - e$; $f$.
**Answer: The king has 13 children.**


**19.** Let's assume that the number $m$ is the square of the two-digit number $x$. The number $m$ ends with the digit 5, and we, therefore, conclude that it is an odd number divisible by 5. Since $m = x \times x$, $x$ must also be an odd number and divisible by 5, which means that it ends with the digit 5. Thus $x = 10a + 5$, where $a$ is a single-digit number.
I. We calculate the squares of all two-digit numbers taking the form $(10a + 5)$ and check the third digit from the end (antepenultimate) of the numbers obtained: $15^2 = 225$, $25^2 = 625$, $35^2 = 1225$, $45^2 = 2025$, $55^2 = 3025$, $65^2 = 4225$, $75^2 = 5625$, $85^2 = 7225$, and $95^2 = 9025$. In each case, the digit is even.
II. We have $m = (10a + 5)^2 = (10a + 5)(10a + 5) = 10a \times 10a + 50a + 50a + 25 = 100(a^2 + a) + 25$, i.e., the antepenultimate digit of the number $m$ is the same as the last digit of the number $(a^2 + a)$. If $a$ is odd, the square of $a$ is also odd, and thus the number $(a^2 + a)$ is even. If, on the other hand, $a$ is even, then $a^2$ is also even, so again the number $(a^2 + a)$ is even. This means that the number $(a^2 + a)$ is always even, and hence the antepenultimate digit of the $m$ number will also be even.
**Answer: The antepenultimate digit of the number $m$ is even.**


**20.** Steve submitted at least 5 problems – if their number had been no more than 4 entries, it would have meant that the remaining schoolchildren submitted 3 problems at most (Steve handed in the most). In such a situation, there would have been no more than $4 + 9 \times 3 = 31$ entries submitted altogether.
It was then possible for Steve to submit exactly 5 problems, because

$35 = 1 + 2 + 3 + 6 \times 4 + 5$ (i.e., one pupil submitted one entry, another two, still another three, six schoolchildren put forward four problems, and Steve submitted five problems on his own).
**Answer: Steve handed in at least 5 problems.**


**21.** Here are a few examples of such sequences:

3, 6, 4, 1, 2, 7, 5        2, 6, 4, 1, 3, 7, 5        5, 7, 2, 1, 4, 3, 6
7, 3, 4, 1, 6, 2, 5        5, 1, 4, 2, 7, 6, 3

We make sure that the above sequences satisfy the conditions stated in the problem by crossing out all possible sets of three numbers (there are 35 such sets).

When we cross out any three numbers, we are left with a four-element sequence, which is neither increasing nor decreasing.

*Note: There are 882 sequences satisfying the conditions defined in the problem.*


**22.** If between 1 and 6, another number is found (e.g., 4), we will get, after crossing out the remaining ones, an increasing or decreasing sequence (e.g., 1, 4, 6, or 6, 4, 1), depending on the order in which the numbers 1 and 6 were written. Otherwise, numbers 1 and 6 would have to have been written side by side.

We have two (non-exclusive) possibilities:

a) The numbers 1 and 6 are followed by at least two numbers $a$, $b$ (in this order). Then, if $a < b$, we leave in the sequence the numbers 1, $a$, $b$, and they form an increasing sequence. If, however, $a > b$, we leave the numbers 6, $a$, $b$, which form a decreasing sequence.

b) Before the numbers 1 and 6 are at least two numbers $a$, $b$ (in this order). Then, if $a < b$, we leave in the sequence the numbers $a$, $b$, 6 so as to have an increasing sequence. If, however, $a > b$, we leave the numbers $a$, $b$, 1 in the sequence, which form a decreasing sequence.

In each case, it is possible to cross out three numbers in such a way that the remaining ones should form either an increasing or decreasing sequence.

**Answer: Agatha is right – it is possible to fulfill the conditions defined in the problem.**

**23.** Let's think for a while how many exams the student could have passed during his first year – we know that the number must be divisible by 3.

a) If the first-year student had passed six exams at most, he would, in the years to come, be sitting less than six examinations per year, and thus he would have passed fewer than $5 \times 6 = 30$ exams altogether. Therefore, the student must have passed more than six exams during his first year.

b) If the student had passed at least 12 exams in his first year, he would, in his final year have passed at least $12 \div 3 = 4$ exams. He would then, during his fourth year, have passed at least five exams, during the third – at least six, and during the second – at least seven. He would have passed at least $12 + 4 + 5 + 6 + 7 = 34$ exams, i.e., the student passed fewer than 12 exams during his first year.

It follows then from subsections a) and b) that the student passed nine exams during his first year and three in his final year. What remains then is $33 – 9 – 3 = 21$ exams falling on the second, third and fourth year of his studies. On the other hand, during his second year, the student passed no more than eight exams, during the third – seven at most, and during the fourth year – six at the very most, and thus $8 + 7 + 6 = 21$ altogether, at most. This means that the student must have passed exactly eight, seven, and six exams during his second, third, and fourth year, respectively.

**Answer: The student passed 7 exams during his third year.**


**24.** Let the three-digit numbers in question have the form: *abc*, *def*, and *ghi*.

The sum of their final digits ($c + f + i$) ends with the digit 5. The sum of three different non-zero one-digit numbers equals at least $1 + 2 + 3 = 6$, and at most $7 + 8 + 9 = 24$. That is why the sum ($c + f + i$) must be equal to 15. In view of the above, $ab0 + de0 + gh0 = 1665 – (c + f + i) = 1650$, therefore, the sum of the digits ($b + e + h$) ends with the digit 5, so it also must be equal to 15. Finally, $1650 = (a + d + g) \times 100 + (b + e + h) \times 10 + (c + f + i) = (a + d + g) \times 100 + 15 \times 10 + 15 = (a + d + g) \times 100 + 165$, hence $a + d + g = 15$.

After the reversal of the first and last digit in the given numbers, we will obtain the following numbers: *cba*, *fed* and *ihg*, which total:

$cba + fed + ihg = (100c + 10b + a) + (100f + 10e + d) + (100i + 10h + g) = 100 (c + f + i) + 10 (b + e + h) + (a + d + g) = 100 \times 15 + 10 \times 15 + 15 = 1665$.

For example, we could have started with these three numbers: 823 + 697 + 145 = 1665; after the reversal of the digits, we would obtain: 328 + 796 + 541 = 1665.
Here are other examples:
469 + 375 + 821 = 1665, and 964 + 573 + 128 = 1665.
**Answer: The sum obtained will also be 1655.**


**25.** Let's represent Bill's cell-phone PIN number by $abcd$. From the conditions stated in the problem, we know that $b = c + d$ and $10a + b + 10c + d = 100$. Substituting $b = c + d$ in the second equation, we obtain $10a + 11c + 2d = 100$. Hence we see that the digit $c$ is even (otherwise the number $(10a + 11c + 2d)$ would be odd and as such could not equal 100).

Moreover, $11c + 2d = 100 - 10a = 10(10 - 10a)$, whence it follows that $(11c + 2d)$ is divisible by 10. We substitute $c$ with consecutive one-digit even numbers and find $d$ such that $(11c + 2d)$ is divisible by 10:

a) $c = 0$, then $d = 0$ or $d = 5$;

b) $c = 2$, then $d = 4$ or $d = 9$;

c) $c = 4$, then $d = 3$ or $d = 8$;

d) $c = 6$, then $d = 2$ or $d = 7$;

e) $c = 8$, then $d = 1$ or $d = 6$.

Solutions in which $c + d \geq 10$ can be rejected straightaway, because it follows from the problem that $c + d = b$ is a one-digit number. We also reject the solution $c = d = 0$, because we cannot then speak of quotient $c$ and $d$.

In the remaining examples, we check the numbers in which the two first and the two last digits constitute two two-digit numbers which add up to 100. We obtain:

a) number 9505 – does not satisfy the required conditions (9 is not the quotient of 0 and 5);

b) number 7624 – does not satisfy the required conditions (7 is not the quotient of 2 and 4);

c) number 5743 – does not satisfy the required conditions (5 is not the quotient of 4 and 3);

d) number 3862 – satisfies all the required conditions ($8 = 6 + 2$, $3 = 6 \div 2$, $38 + 62 = 100$);

e) number 1981 – does not satisfy the required conditions (1 is not the quotient of 8 and 1).

**Answer: Bill's cellular phone PIN number is 3862.**

# CHAPTER 2

## DIVISIBILITY AND PRIME NUMBERS

**26.** If the last digit of Mr. Wilson's year of his birth was smaller than 9, the sum of the digits of the husband's and the wife's birth years would differ by 1, so at least one of the sums would be indivisible by 4. Thus Mr. Wilson must have been born in a year ending with 9. In the 20$^{th}$ century, only the years 1919, 1959, and 1999 have the sum of their digits divisible by 4. Therefore, Mrs. Wilson could have been born in 1920, 1960, or 2000, of which only the first two numbers have the sum of their respective digits divisible by 4.
**Answer: Mr. Wilson was born either in 1919 or in 1959.**

**27.** The age of each son is the divisor of the number 30. Let's enumerate all the natural divisors of the number 30 and denote them by $d$: 1, 2, 3, 5, 6, 10, 15, and 30. Among the divisors, one should choose three (not necessarily different, for Mr. Triangle could have twins) whose product equals 30 and whose sum is 12. Let's consider possible values of $d$ starting with the greatest among the chosen divisors.
a) If $d = 15$ or $d = 30$, then the sum of three divisors will be equal to at least 15, which means too much.
b) If $d = 10$, then we must assume the remaining two divisors to be 1 and 1 (so that the sum equals 12), but then $10 \times 1 \times 1 = 10 \neq 30$.
c) If $d = 6$, the sum of the two remaining divisors must equal 6, i.e., they must be either 5 and 1, or 3 and 3. The product equal to 30 will be obtained only in the first case: $6 \times 5 \times 1 = 30$.
d) If $d = 5$, the sum of the two remaining divisors must equal 7; in which case, they will be 5 and 2, but $5 \times 5 \times 2 = 50 \neq 30$.
e) If $d \leq 3$, the product of three divisors will at most equal $3 \times 3 \times 3 = 27 < 30$.
**Answer: Mr. Triangle's sons are one, five, and six years old.**

**28.** Please note that $BBB = B \times 111 = B \times 3 \times 37$, i.e., the right side of our equality is divisible by 37 and by 3. Therefore, the left side must also be divisible by 37, which is possible only when 37 is the divisor of the number *AB*. There are, therefore, two possibilities: either *AB* = 37 or *AB* = 74. For *A* = 3 and *B* = 7, the left side equals 37 × 3 × 7 = 111 × 7 = 777, i.e., equal to the right side of the equality. In the second case, the left side of the equation is equal to 74 × 7 × 4; therefore, it is not divisible by 3, and so it is not equal to the right side of the equality.

**Answer: A = 3 and B = 7.**


**29.** If the dragon has more than seven heads, then after it has had seven heads cut off, one of them grows back, and their number decreases by 6. Assuming that the knight cuts off seven heads at a time, 16 times in a row, the dragon will be left with 100 − 16 × 6 = 4 heads. Then, the knight can cut off just one head which will result in the growth of four new heads, i.e., the dragon will have 7 heads. As this is the number the knight can cut off with one stroke, we see that he can kill the beast.

Let's assume now that the dragon has 99 heads. The knight can increase the number of dragon heads by 3 (if he cuts off just one head) or decrease by 6 (if he cuts off seven or eleven heads). Since the dragon has initially 99 heads, the number of heads left will always be divisible by 3 as long as he is alive. With one stroke of his sword, the knight cannot possibly cut off a number of heads divisible by 3 (the numbers 1, 7, and 11 are not divisible by 3), which means that he cannot kill the dragon.

**Answer: It is possible to kill a hundred-headed dragon. However, if the dragon had 99 heads, it would be impossible for the knight to slay him.**


# 30.

Method I:

Since $376^2 = 141,376,376^2$ ends with digits 376. To make sure whether $376^3$ also ends with the same three digits, we can multiply $376^2 = 141,376$ by 376. As we are interested only in the final three digits of the product of 141,376 × 376, it is sufficient to multiply the last three digits of the number 141,376 (i.e., 376) by 376, because only the three-digit endings of the factors are decisive about the last three digits of their product (this is clearly seen when we perform a multiplication in writing). We have already established that 376 × 376 = 141,376 ends with the digits 376, and thus $376^3$ will also end with the same digits.

By extension: $376^4 = 376^3 \times 376 = ...376 \times 376$, and the obtained product has the same last three digits as the product from $376 \times 376 = 141,376$; therefore, $376^4$ also ends with the digits 376.

Method II:
In a more formal notation, the number $376^3$ takes the form of $1000k + 376$. We have thus $376^4 = 376^3 \times 376 = (1000k + 376) \times 376 = 1000 \times 376k + 141,376 = 1000 \times 376k + 141,000 + 376 = 1000 \times (376k + 141) + 376$, i.e., $376^4$ also ends with the digits 376.
**Answer: The proposition submitted here is true.**

**31.** When a column of fours had been formed of plastic troops, there were only three soldiers left in the last row of the column, which means that the total number of plastic soldiers is odd.
After the soldiers have been arranged in a column of sixes, they will be marching side by side in threes:

| | |
|---|---|
| ✱ ✱ ✱ ✱ ✱ ✱ | six soldiers |
| ✱ ✱ ✱ ✱ ✱ ✱ | six soldiers |
| ✱ ✱ ✱ ✱ ✱ ✱ | six soldiers |
| ✱ ✱ | last (incomplete) row |

or

| | |
|---|---|
| ✱ ✱ ✱ ✱ ✱ ✱ | six soldiers |
| ✱ ✱ ✱ ✱ ✱ ✱ | six soldiers |
| ✱ ✱ ✱ ✱ ✱ ✱ | six soldiers |
| ✱ ✱ ✱ ✱ ✱ | last (incomplete) row |

When a column of threes has been formed, there will only be two soldiers in the last row; therefore, when we decide to form a column of sixes, the last row will include two soldiers or $2 + 3 = 5$ soldiers. Since we know that the total number of plastic figures is odd, we cannot possibly have 2 soldiers in the last row.
**Answer: When we form a column of sixes of plastic troops, we will be left with five soldiers.**

**32.** The first of four digits is 1, which means that the product of the remaining three is 12. Let's proceed with the full factorization of the number 12 using three one-digit factors: $12 = 1 \times 2 \times 6$, or $12 = 1 \times 3 \times 4$, or 12 = 2 × 2 × 3. In the first case, the sum of all four digits of the year equals 1 + 1 + 2 + 6 = 10 and is not divisible by 9; thus the whole number is not divisible by 9, and even less so by 27 = 3 × 9. That is why we discard this case. Similarly, in the third example, the sum of digits 1 + 2 + 2 + 3 = 8 is indivisible by 9, so we also ignore it. Therefore, the sought year must be a number consisting of the following digits: 1, 1, 3, and 4. Since it is an odd number beginning with 1, we are faced with four combinations: 1143, 1341, 1413, or 1431. Among these four, the only one divisible by 27 is 1431.

**Answer: Joan of Arc died at the stake in 1431.**


**33.** We find quite easily 3 numbers with the required condition, e.g., 1, 2, and 3 – their sum equals 6 and is divisible by 1, 2, and 3. We want to add a fourth number $A$ such that all four numbers will satisfy the condition stated. The sum 1 + 2 + 3 + $A$ = 6 + $A$ must be divisible by 1, 2, and 3, i.e., by 6. Therefore, $A$ must also be divisible by 6. Moreover, (6 + $A$) must be divisible by $A$, which means that 6 = (6 + $A$) – $A$ must also be divisible by $A$. For this reason, $A$ must be equal to 6.

Sure enough, the numbers 1, 2, 3 and 6 answer the required condition, i.e., their sum (equal to 12) is divisible by each of these numbers.

As our next step, we add to these four numbers the fifth one in such a way that all the five numbers should satisfy the required conditions. Reasoning in an analogous way, we can convince ourselves that we need to add the number 12, etc.

We finally obtain 10 numbers: 1, 2, 3, 6, 12, 24, 48, 96, 192, and 384, whose sum is 768 and is divisible by each of the numbers above.

**Answer: It is possible to find 10 numbers satisfying the required conditions.**


**34.** If $n > 5$ is an even natural number, we can represent it in the form of the sum: $n = 2 + (n - 2)$, where 2 is a prime number, and $(n - 2)$ is an even number greater than 5 – 2 = 3; so $(n - 2)$ is a complex number.

If, however, $n > 5$ is an odd natural number, we can write it as the following sum: $n = 3 + (n - 3)$, where 3 is a prime number, and $(n - 3)$ is an odd number greater than 5 – 3 = 2; so $(n - 3)$ is a complex number.

**Answer: Yes, each natural number greater than 5 can be put in the form of such a sum.**

**35.** Let's assume that $d$ is a common divisor of the numbers $a_1, a_2, a_3, \ldots$, and $a_{49}$. In that case, $d$ is the divisor of the sum $a_1 + a_2 + a_3 + \ldots + a_{49}$, so it divides $999 = 27 \times 37$.
On the other hand, we have $a_1 \geq d, a_2 \geq d, a_3 \geq d, \ldots, a_{49} \geq d$,
hence $999 = a_1 + a_2 + a_3 + \ldots + a_{49} \geq 49d$,
i.e., $d \leq \frac{999}{49} = 20 + \frac{19}{49}$ .
The only divisors of the number 999 no greater than 20 are 1, 3, and 9, which means that the greatest common divisor of the numbers $a_1, a_2, a_3, \ldots, a_{49}$ may equal to 1, 3, or 9.
Let's consider three possibilities:
a) If we take $a_1 = a_2 = a_3 = \ldots = a_{48} = 9$,
then $a_{49} = 999 - 48 \times 9 = 567$. Hence $a_1 + a_2 + a_3 + \ldots + a_{49} = 999$ and numbers $a_1, a_2, a_3, \ldots$, and $a_{49}$ have the greatest common divisor equal to 9.
b) If we assume that $a_1 = a_2 = a_3 = \ldots = a_{48} = 3$,
then $a_{49} = 999 - 48 \times 3 = 855$. Hence $a_1 + a_2 + a_3 + \ldots + a_{49} = 999$ and the greatest common divisor of numbers $a_1, a_2, a_3, \ldots$, and $a_{49}$ is equal to 3.
c) If we assume $a_1 = a_2 = a_3 = \ldots = a_{48} = 1$, then $a_{49} = 999 - 48 \times 1 = 851$. Hence $a_1 + a_2 + a_3 + \ldots + a_{49} = 999$ and the numbers $a_1, a_2, a_3, \ldots, a_{49}$ have the greatest common divisor equal to 1.
**Answer: The greatest common divisor of numbers $a_1, a_2, a_3, \ldots$, and $a_{49}$ can be equal to 1, 3, or 9.**


**36.** Let's assume $a$, $b$, and $c$ to be any three numbers among the chosen seven. Then by assumption, 7 is a divisor of numbers $(a + b)$ and $(b + c)$, and therefore, is also the divisor of their sum $(a + b) + (b + c) = (a + 2b + c)$. In addition and also by assumption, the number $(a + c)$ is divisible by 7, which means in turn that it also divides the difference of numbers $(a + 2b + c)$ and $(a + c)$, i.e., $2b$ is divisible by 7. Since 7 and 2 are co-prime (relatively prime), 7 is the divisor of the number $b$. Numbers $(a + b)$ and $b$ are divisible by 7, i.e., their difference has the same property $(a + b) - b = a$. Similarly, 7 is the divisor of numbers $(b + c)$ and $b$, i.e., 7 is also the divisor of $(b + c) - b = c$. We have, therefore, demonstrated that if $a$, $b$ and $c$ are any three numbers among the chosen seven numbers, then each of the numbers $a$, $b$, and $c$ is divisible by 7. Therefore, each of the seven chosen numbers is divisible by 7.
**Answer: All the chosen numbers are divisible by 7.**

# 37.

**Method I:**

Let the notation of such a year take the form of $abcd$. We know from the initial conditions that $ab + cd = bc$ and $ab \geq 20$. Hence we obtain $bc \geq 20$, i.e., $b \geq 2$, and consequently $ab \geq 22$. Since we are searching for the nearest exceptional year after the year 2006, let's substitute 22 for $ab$ and try to find the solution. We then have $22 + cd = 20 + c$, which is impossible because $22 + cd > 20 + cd \geq 20 + c$.

We, therefore, conclude that $ab \geq 23$. Let's now put in $ab = 23$; hence we have $23 + cd = 30 + c$. We are looking for the minimum values meeting the condition $\geq 2006$. We begin from the smallest possible value for $c = 0$. In that case, $23 + d = 30$, i.e., $d = 7$, which yields the answer: 2307.

**Method II:**

A reader with an enquiring mind could ask a question about the total number of all the exceptional years and would want to list them. The answer boils down to finding digits $a$, $b$, $c$, and $d$, such that $10a + b + + 10c + d = 10b + c$, and after transformation: $10a + d = 9(b - c)$. The number $(10a + d)$ is positive, which means that $b > c$; to simplify the notation, we adopt $ad$ instead of $(10a + d)$.

At this point, we will test all possible values of the difference $b - c$:

a) $b - c = 0$; $ad = 0$, which is an impossible case.

b) $b - c = 1$; $ad = 9$, which is an impossible case.

c) $b - c = 2$; $ad = 18$, which gives eight possible results: 1208, 1318, 1428, 1538, 1648, 1758, 1868, 1979.

d) $b - c = 3$; $ad = 27$, which gives seven possible results: 2307, 2417, 2527, 2637, 2747, 2857, 2967.

e) $b - c = 4$; $ad = 36$, which yields six results: 3406, 3516, 3626, 3736, 3846, 3956.

f) $b - c = 5$; $ad = 45$, which yields five possible answers: 4505, 4615, 4725, 4835, 4945.

g) $b - c = 6$; $ad = 54$, which yields four possible answers: 5604, 5714, 5824, 5934.

h) $b - c = 7$; $ad = 63$, which gives three possible answers: 6703, 6813, 6923.

i) $b - c = 8$; $ad = 72$, which gives two possible answers: 7802, 7912.

j) $b - c = 9$; $ad = 81$, which gives one possible answer: 8901.

The number of all exceptional four-digit years will be then equal to the sum: $8 + 7 + 6 + 5 + 4 + 3 + 2 + 1 = 36$, and 2307 is the nearest year sought.

**Answer: The nearest exceptional year after 2006 is the year 2307.**

**38.** Please note that the square of the natural number $n$ when divided by 4 always gives a remainder of 0 or 1. Surely enough, there are actually four possibilities:

a) $n$ yields a remainder of 0 when divided by 4, i.e., it takes the form of $n = 4k$ for a certain natural $k$. In that case, $n^2 = (4k)^2 = 4k \times 4k = 4 \times 4k^2$ yields a remainder of 0 when it is divided by 4.

b) $n$ yields a remainder of 1 when divided by 4, i.e., it takes the form of $n = 4k + 1$ for a certain natural $k$. In that case, $n^2 = (4k + 1)(4k + 1) = = 4k \times 4k + 4k + 4k + 1 = 4 \times (4k^2 + 2k) + 1$ yields a remainder of 1 when divided by 4.

c) $n$ yields a remainder of 2 when divided by 4, i.e., it takes the form of $n = 4k + 2$ for a certain natural $k$. In that case, $n^2 = (4k + 2)(4k + 2) = = 4k \times 4k + 8k + 8k + 4 = 4 \times (4k^2 + 4k + 1)$ yields a remainder of 0 when divided by 4.

d) $n$ yields a remainder of 3 when divided by 4, i.e., it takes the form of $n = 4k + 3$ for a certain natural $k$. In that case, $n^2 = (4k + 3)(4k + 3) = = 4k \times 4k + 12k + 12k + 9 = 4 \times (4k^2 + 6k + 2) + 1$ yields a remainder of 1 when divided by 4.

What we have is $2006 = 4 \times 501 + 2$, i.e., $(a^2 + 2006)$ when divided by 4 always yields a remainder of 2 or 3; so it is not a square of a natural number.

**Answer: There is no natural number satisfying the conditions stated.**

# 39.

a) Let's introduce in the table the remainders after the division of the number $(2a + 1)$ by 7 as a function of the remainder when the number $a$ is divided by 7:

| Remainder after the division of $a$ by 7 | Remainder after the division of $(2a + 1)$ by 7 |
|---|---|
| 0 | 1 |
| 1 | 3 |
| 2 | 5 |
| 3 | 0 |
| 4 | 2 |
| 5 | 4 |
| 6 | 6 |

Let's, for example, check one of the rows in the table. If $a$ yields a remainder of 5 after being divided by 7, then $a = 7k + 5$ for a certain natural $k$, i.e., $2a + 1 = 2 \times (7k + 5) + 1 = 14k + 11 = 7 \times (2k + 1) + 4$

gives a remainder of 4 when divided by 7. We check the remaining six rows in the same way.

It follows from the above table that the remainders after division change in subsequent operations according to the following patterns: $0 \to 1 \to 3 \to 0$, $2 \to 5 \to 4 \to 2$ and $6 \to 6$.

This means that if we start with a number whose remainder after division by 7 equals for example 1, then after subsequent operations, we will obtain numbers with remainders equaling: 3, 0, 1, 3, 0, 1, 3, 0, 1, 3, ...

Let's check what number we should start with to obtain after five operations a number divisible by 7 (i.e., with a remainder of 0):

$1 \to 3 \to 0 \to 1 \to 3 \to 0 \to 1 \to 3 \to 0 \to 1 \to 3 \to 0 \to ...$

If we begin with a number which after division by 7 yields a remainder of 1, then after performing five operations, we will obtain a number divisible by 7.

$(1 \to 3 \to 0 \to 1 \to 3 \to 0)$.

Here is an example. We begin with 1, and after subsequent operations, we obtain: 3, 7, 15, 31, and 63. The number 63, the result after five operations, is divisible by 7.

b) After each such operation, we obtain an odd number, so the final result is indivisible by 12.

**Answer: The final result can be a number divisible by 7, but cannot be divisible by 12.**


**40.** Please note that the sum $1 + 2 + 3 + ... + 110 = (1 + 2) + (3 + 4) + (5 + 6) + ... + (109 + 110)$ is an odd number, because it is the sum of 55 odd terms. Let's demonstrate that if the sum of the numbers written on the blackboard is odd, then it will remain so, whichever our next move may be. There are two possibilities:

a) The sum of the two crossed out numbers is odd. Hence one of them is even, and the other one is odd, i.e., their difference is odd. This means that we eliminate two numbers whose sum is odd and replace them with an odd one instead, i.e., the sum of numbers written on the blackboard will remain odd.

b) The sum of the two canceled numbers is even. Hence both these numbers are either even or odd, so their difference is even. This means that we cross out two numbers whose sum is even, and instead of them, we write an even number; therefore, the sum of numbers written on the blackboard will remain odd.

In the beginning, the sum of the numbers written on the blackboard was odd, and it will remain so, after each round. If the number ten remained on the blackboard, then the sum of the numbers on the blackboard would equal 10, i.e., it would be even, which is impossible.
**Answer: The number remaining on the blackboard could not have equaled 10.**

# CHAPTER 3

## EQUATIONS

**41.** For every cast equal to a one, Simon is given 50 cents with which he pays back Tom for five casts in which other values come out. So in order to have a situation where neither owes the other anything, a one must fall on every six throws. On $30 = 5 \times 6$ throws, a one must have fallen 5 times, and other values must have fallen 25 times.
**Answer: A one came out five times.**

**42.**
Method I:
If each family that have three bicycles, give away one of their bicycles to those possessing only one bicycle, then each family in the village will have two bicycles. Therefore, there are in total $29 \times 2 = 58$ bicycles in the village.

Method II:
We represent by $a$ the number of families having one bicycle and by $b$ those families who have two bicycles, while the number of families with three bicycles is also represented by $a$.
What we have then is $a + b + a = 29$, and the number of bicycles in the village is:
$1 \times a + 2 \times b + 3 \times a = 4a + 2b = 2(a + b + a) = 2 \times 29 = 58.$
**Answer: There are 58 bicycles in the village.**

**43.** William came fifth or did even better, and he ended up exactly in the middle of results list, which means that there were at most 9 contenders. On the other hand, Paul came eighth or worse, and it was the penultimate place, which means that there were at least 9 boys taking part.
**Answer: 9 boys took part in the long jump event.**

**44.** During 8 hours, the father will have dug $\frac{8}{12} = \frac{2}{3}$ of the plot of land. The son, however, in eight hours can dig $1 - \frac{2}{3} = \frac{1}{3}$ of the plot, i.e., the son works half as fast as his father. Hence the conclusion is that he will take $2 \times 12 = 24$ to dig the entire plot of land.
**Answer: The son will take 24 hours to dig the plot.**

**45.** Let the time for Daniel to cover a distance of one meter be denoted by unit $d$.
Daniel will take $3d$ to creep the whole distance, and Sebastian $\frac{1}{2}d + 1d + 2d = 3\frac{1}{2}d$. This means that Daniel will win. When the winner crosses the finish line, Sebastian will have covered the first two sections in $\frac{3}{2}d$ and a portion of the third leg of the race in $\frac{3}{2}d$ at a speed of $\frac{1}{2}$ meter per time unit. He will have covered $\frac{3}{2} \times \frac{1}{2} = \frac{3}{4}$ m of the final leg of the race, i.e., he will still have $\frac{1}{4}$ m to go to complete the race.
**Answer: The winner will be Daniel, who will best his opponent by $\frac{1}{4}$ of a meter.**

**46.** Since each child was given the same number of identical cakes, the brothers must have bought the same number of cakes of each kind as well. Three cakes (cream cake + fruit cake + doughnut) cost $1 + \frac{1}{2} + \frac{1}{3} = \frac{11}{6}$ dollars, i.e., Jeremy and Roger bought six sets of three cakes each. Six sets of three cakes can be shared by one, two, three or six kids.
We know for sure, however, that among the children were two boys, Jeremy and Roger, which means that in the group were also a minimum of two girls.
There were, therefore, at least four kids apart from Jeremy and Roger.
**Answer: The group numbered 6 kids.**

**47.** The amount the first boy gave did not exceed what the remaining two boys chipped in, so he gave no more than half of the whole sum, i.e., at most $22.50. If the second boy paid $a$ dollars, then the remaining two boys contributed at least $2a$, and so all the three boys gave at least $3a altogether. This means that $45 \geq 3a$, i.e., the second boy paid in $45 \div 3 = $15, at most. Similarly, if the third boy gave $b$, then the remaining two added at least $5b$, i.e., all the boys gave at least $6b$. It follows from the above that $45 \geq 6a$, i.e., the third boy chipped in $45 \div 6 = $7.50, at most.

Let's verify: $22.50 + $15 + $7.50 = $45, so if the first boy had given less than $22.50, the second one less than $15 and the third less than $7.50, they wouldn't have collected $45 altogether.

**Answer: The first boy chipped in $22.50, the second $15, and the third $7.50.**

**48.** Ken runs up the escalator in the opposite direction of the movement of the stairs, so he moves at the same speed as his cap on the neighboring escalator. This means that Ken will be able to get hold of his cap only when he reaches the top of the escalator – precisely at the same moment as his cap finds itself there. To catch it, Ken must cover half the length of the stairs.

Will, on the other hand, to get to the top, must first cover half the length of the stairs, (at a speed three times as high as that of Ken, because he will be running in the same direction as the escalator), and then run up the whole length of the neighboring stairs (in the same direction as the escalator, again three times as fast as Ken). He has to cover $\frac{3}{2}$ of the length of the escalator, i.e., three times as far as his friend, but three times as fast. Hence the conclusion is that the boys will meet at the top of the stairs at the same time as the cap.

**Answer: The boys will reach the cap simultaneously.**

**49.** By starting to run from the new line, Andrew has to cover a distance of 120 m. He takes as much time to cover 100 m as Dave to run 80 m. Hence the conclusion is that Andrew, beginning 20 meters earlier, will draw level with Dave after covering 100 m, and will overtake him in the last 20 m. Joe is wrong then.

Please note that covering 25 meters takes Andrew as much time as Dave

needs to run 20 meters. This means that Andrew will cover the distance of $5 \times 25$ m $= 125 = 100 + 25$ m in the same time as Dave $5 \times 20 = 100$ m.
**Answer: Joe is not right. The new line should be drawn 25 meters before the official starting line.**

# 50.

Method I:
It follows from the table that Sophie (S), Adam (A), Michael (M) and Will (W) make up $\frac{1}{2} - \frac{1}{3} = \frac{1}{6}$ of schoolchildren in Class 5B i.e. the class numbers $4 \times 6 = 24$ children.

| Group 1 | | | Group 2 | | | |
|---|---|---|---|---|---|---|
| | | S | A | M | W | |
| $\frac{1}{3}$ | | | | | | $\frac{1}{2}$ |

Method II:
Let's call $x$ the number of schoolchildren in the first group. There are $3(x - 1)$ children in the class, because after Sophie left group 1 for group 2, in the first group remains $\frac{1}{3}$ of the class. We know as well that together with Adam, Michael and Will, the first group makes up half of the class, i.e., the number of schoolchildren in Class 5B is also equal to $2(x + 3)$. Therefore, $3(x - 1) = 2(x + 3)$, hence $x = 9$. The number of children at school is then equal to $3(x - 1) = 3 \times 8 = 24$.
**Answer: Class 5B has 24 children.**

**51.** The sum of the numerator and denominator for each of the listed fractions equals 2008. Among the fractions, there is also $\frac{1004}{1004} = 1$. We can, therefore, select three fractions, e.g., $\frac{2}{2006}$, $\frac{1004}{1004}$, $\frac{2006}{2}$ whose product is 1.
**Answer: Yes, it is possible to find fractions satisfying the set conditions.**

**52.** Let's calculate:

$$\frac{124\,124}{421\,421} = \frac{124 \times 1000 + 124}{421 \times 1000 + 421} = \frac{124 \times 1001}{421 \times 1001} = \frac{124}{421},$$

$$\frac{1240\,124}{4210\,421} = \frac{124 \times 10\,000 + 124}{421 \times 10\,000 + 421} = \frac{124 \times 10\,001}{421 \times 10\,001} = \frac{124}{421}.$$

**Answer: The numbers listed above are equal.**

**53.** We have:

$$\frac{1}{(10 \times 11)} = \frac{(11-10)}{(10 \times 11)} = \frac{1}{10} - \frac{1}{11}, \quad \frac{1}{(11 \times 12)} = \frac{(12-11)}{(11 \times 12)} = \frac{1}{11} - \frac{1}{12}, \dots, \frac{1}{(19 \times 20)} =$$

$$= \frac{(20-19)}{(19 \times 20)} = \frac{1}{19} - \frac{1}{20}.$$

Hence:

$$\frac{1}{(10 \times 11)} + \frac{1}{(11 \times 12)} + \dots + \frac{1}{(19 \times 20)} = (\frac{1}{10} - \frac{1}{11}) + (\frac{1}{11} - \frac{1}{12}) + (\frac{1}{12} - \frac{1}{13}) + \dots +$$

$$+ (\frac{1}{18} - \frac{1}{19}) + (\frac{1}{19} - \frac{1}{20}) = \frac{1}{10} + (-\frac{1}{11} + \frac{1}{11}) + (-\frac{1}{12} + \frac{1}{12}) + \dots + (-\frac{1}{19} + \frac{1}{19}) - \frac{1}{20} =$$

$$= \frac{1}{10} - \frac{1}{20} = \frac{1}{20}.$$

**54.** Let's have a look at the number of watermelons just before the appearance of the last buyer. If Ms. Cindy had bought only half of the remaining watermelons, Catherine would have been left with a melon and a half. So Catherine had 3 watermelons before Ms. Cindy arrived. Similarly, before Ms. Barbara's arrival, she had $2 \times (3 + 0.5) = 7$ watermelons, and before Ms. Angela showed up, she had $2 \times (7 + 0.5) = 15$ watermelons. Catherine sold then 14 melons, earning $14 \times 2 = \$28$.
**Answer: Catherine's takings amounted to \$28.**

**55.** Let's define by $x$ the initial number of rabbits. The first customer bought $(\frac{1}{6}x + 1)$ bunnies, so the breeder was left with $(\frac{5}{6}x - 1)$. The second customer bought $(\frac{1}{6}(\frac{5}{6}x - 1) + 2)$ rabbits, but we know that he purchased as many bunnies as the previous buyer. Therefore, $\frac{1}{6}(\frac{5}{6}x - 1) + 2 = \frac{1}{6}x + 1$, hence $(\frac{5}{6}x - 1) + 12 = x + 6$, i.e., $5 = \frac{1}{6}x$.
In the beginning, the breeder must have had 30 rabbits.
Let's check now whether all the customers bought the same number of bunnies.
The first customer bought $\frac{1}{6} \times 30 + 1 = 6$ rabbits – there remained 24 animals.
The second customer bought $\frac{1}{6} \times 24 + 2 = 6$ rabbits – there remained 18 animals.
The third customer bought $\frac{1}{6} \times 18 + 3 = 6$ rabbits – there remained 12 animals.
The fourth customer bought $\frac{1}{6} \times 12 + 4 = 6$ rabbits – there remained 6 animals.

The fifth customer bought $\frac{1}{6} \times 6 + 5 = 6$ rabbits – there remained 0 animals.

We see then that each customer bought the same number of rabbits (six).

**Answer: The rabbit breeder had brought to the market 30 animals and had 5 customers that day.**

**56.** Consecutive sheep eat hay at a rate of $1, \frac{1}{2}, \frac{1}{3}, \dots$, and $\frac{1}{8}$ portion per day. Thus the first two sheep eat $1 + \frac{1}{2} = \frac{3}{2}$ portions of hay daily, whereas the remaining six eat $\frac{1}{3} + \frac{1}{4} + \frac{1}{5} + \frac{1}{6} + \frac{1}{7} + \frac{1}{8}$ portions. We have $\frac{1}{3} + \frac{1}{4} + \frac{1}{5} + \frac{1}{6} + \frac{1}{7} + \frac{1}{8} = (\frac{1}{3} + \frac{1}{6}) + (\frac{1}{4} + \frac{1}{5} + \frac{1}{7} + \frac{1}{8}) <$ $< \frac{1}{2} + (\frac{1}{4} + \frac{1}{4} + \frac{1}{4} + \frac{1}{4}) = \frac{3}{2}$ (note: we have used obvious inequalities: $\frac{1}{5} < \frac{1}{4}, \frac{1}{7} < \frac{1}{4}, \frac{1}{8} < \frac{1}{4}$). This means that the last six sheep eat hay at a smaller total rate than the first two animals.

**Answer: The first two sheep will eat their hay faster.**

**57.** Let's assume that at first Michael had $d$ dollars and $c$ cents on him, i.e., $100d + c$ cents. It follows from the problem that $c$ is an even number, and $c < 100$. After a quarter of an hour, Michael had $100 \times \frac{c}{2} + d$ cents, which equaled half of the initial sum.

Thus $100 \times \frac{c}{2} + d = \frac{100d + c}{2}$, i.e., $= 99c = 98d$.

Since 99 and 98 are relatively prime numbers, 99 is a divisor of $d$ and 98 is a divisor of $c$. We know that $c$ is a natural number smaller than 100, hence $c = 0$ or $c = 98$. For $c = 0$, we obtain $d = 0$ as well. From the problem, we know, however, that Michael had some money on him since he spent half of it, and that is why we reject this case as impossible.

What remains is $c = 98$, and then from equation $99c = 98d$, we obtain $d = 99$.

Let's check: If Michael came to the market with $99.98, then after a quarter of an hour, he was left with half of it, i.e., $49.99. Sure enough, after a quarter of an hour, the number of cents (99) equals the number of dollars in the beginning, and the number of dollars (49) is now half of the initial number of cents (98).

**Answer: Initially Michael had $99.98 on him.**

**58.** If we express by $D$, $M$, $J$, and $P$ the number of years of Dave, Mark, Jack, and Paul, respectively, we will be able to form equalities: $J = M + 4 = D + 8$, and $M \times P = J \times D + 16$.

From the first equality, we have $J = M + 4$, and $D = M - 4$. Substituting these in the equation $M \times P = J \times D + 16$, we obtain $M \times P = (M + 4) \times (M - 4) + 16$, i.e. $M \times P = M^2$.

We obtain the equality $M(P - M) = 0$, from which it follows that $P = M$, because $M$ cannot equal zero. Thus the twins are Mark and Paul. No other pair of boys can be twins, because $J > M > D$, $J > P$ (it results from $P = M$), and $P > D$.

**Answer: In the foursome mentioned above, the twins are Mark and Paul.**

**59.** We designate the sum written on the check – $d$ for dollars and $c$ for cents, where $c$ is a natural number smaller than 100. Let's express the amount on the check in numbers of cents and as follows: $(100d + c)$. But the cashier paid out instead $(100c + d)$ cents. It follows from the contents of the problem that $d$ is also a natural number smaller than 100. We also know that the sum paid out and diminished by 5 cents equals $2(100d + c)$. We obtain then the equation $100c + d - 5 = 2(100d + c)$, hence $98c - 5 = 199d$, i.e., $98(c - 2d) = 5 + 3d$.

The left-hand side of the last equation is divisible by 98, which means that the right-hand side must also be divisible by this number. Since $d \leq 99$, $5 + 3d \leq 302$, the only possible solutions are: $5 + 3d = 0$, or $5 + 3d = 98$, or $5 + 3d = 2 \times 98$, or $5 + 3d = 3 \times 98$. Solving these equations, we will note that we obtain a non-finite value $d$ in all cases, but the second. That is why the only correct solution is the second case, i.e., $5 + 3d = 98$, hence $d = 31$. On this basis and from the equation $98(c - 2d) = 5 + 3d$, we calculate $c = 63$.

**Answer: Michael's check amounted to \$31.63.**

**60.** The number of pairs is even, i.e., the total number of pupils is divisible by 4. Therefore, the number of girls can equal 2, 6, or 10. The number of twosomes consisting of a boy and girl equals the number of all the children divided by 4, i.e., it is 4, 5, or 6.

a) If there were only 2 girls, we could not possibly have as many as 4 mixed pairs.

b) If there were 6 girls, then we would have 5 such pairs, which means that the sixth girl would also have to form a pair with a boy and that would make six mixed pairs, i.e., more than any other remaining pairs.

c) If there were 10 girls, then there would be six mixed pairs. The remaining six twos would comprise two pairs of girls and four pairs of boys.

**Answer: Class 5A has 24 schoolchildren.**

**61.** Let $x$ be the age of Anna in years. Since $24 = 2 \times 12$, Anna was 12 years old when Maria was as old as Anna is now. This simply means that Anna was 12 when Maria was $x$ years of age. Now Anna is $x$ years old, and Maria is 24. Since the difference in their ages remains constant, $12 - x = x - 24$; hence $x = 18$.

**Answer: Anna is 18 years old.**

**62.** Let's mark by $x$ the present age of granny and by $y$ the age of grandpa. We know from the problem that $(y - x)$ years ago grandpa was as old as granny is now. Before $(y - x)$ years, granny was $x - (y - x)$ years old. Grandpa is now twice as old as Granny was then, i.e., the present age of grandpa is $2(x - (y - x))$ years. Therefore, $y = 2(x - (y - x)) = 2(2x - y) = 4x - 2y$, i.e., $3y = 4x$.

We also know that the sum of their ages is 140 years, so $x + y = 140$, and hence $y = 140 - x$. Substituting the latter in the equation $3y = 4x$, we obtain $3(140 - x) = 4x$, so $3 \times 140 = 7x$, i.e., $x = 3 \times 20 = 60$.

**Answer: Granny is now 60 years old.**

**63.** Let's assume that $j$, $a$ and $f$ denote the number of mushrooms collected by Joe, Alex, and Frank, respectively. We have $j + a = 3f$ and $a + f = 5j$. After adding the respective two sides together, we obtain $f + j + 2a = 3f + 5j$, hence $2a = 2f + 4j$, i.e., $a = f + 2j$. We assume at the same time that $j > 0$, because otherwise it would follow from the equation $a + f = 5j$ that nobody found a single mushroom.

Therefore, $a = f + 2j > f + j$.

**Answer: Alex found more mushrooms than Joe and Frank together.**

**64.** When Len loses, we multiply the sum of the money he has by $\frac{1}{2}$, and when he wins by $\frac{3}{2}$. Since this is both a commutative and associative multiplication, the sequence of Len's wins and losses does not make a difference. After four wins and three losses, he will be left with a sum of money equal to the initial amount multiplied by $(\frac{3}{2})^4$ and multiplied by $(\frac{1}{2})^3$, i.e., $32 \times (\frac{3}{2})^4 \times (\frac{1}{2})^3 = 32 \times \frac{81}{128} = \frac{81}{4} = 20\frac{1}{4}$.

**Answer: Len has 20 dollars and 25 cents now.**

**65.** Let's assume that each digit occurs in this number $p$ times. Then, the sum of digits in this number equals $(0 + 1 + 2 + 3 + 4 + 5 + 6 + 7 + 8 + 9) \times p = 45p$ and is divisible by 3. Therefore, the whole number is divisible by 3, i.e., it cannot be a power of 2.

**Answer: The number in question cannot be a power of 2.**


**66.** We assume that the radius of the hole in the middle of the wheel is our unit of measurement, i.e., $u = \frac{11}{7}$ in. Then, the radius of the wheel is $11 = 7 \times \frac{11}{7}$ in, i.e., $7u$. The area of the wheel with a radius of $7u$ and a hole cut out in the centre with the radius $u$ equals $\pi \times 7^2 - \pi \times 1^2 = 48\,\pi(u^2)$. Let's mark by $R$ the new radius of the used wheel expressed in units $u$ when the grinding wheel is handed over to Michael. The area of the wheel with radius $R$ which has an opening of radius 1 cut out in its center equals half of $48\pi(u^2)$, i.e., $\pi(R^2 - 1) = 24\,\pi(u^2)$, hence $R^2 = 25(u^2)$, i.e., $R = 5u$. So the diameter of the wheel when it goes to Michael will be equal to $2 \times 5u = 2 \times 5 \times \frac{11}{7} = \frac{110}{7} = 15\frac{5}{7}$ in.

**Answer: The diameter of the grinding wheel will equal $15\frac{5}{7}$ inches.**


# CHAPTER 4

## GEOMETRY


**67.** Since the distance between $D$ and $E$ is the same as the sum of distances between $D$ and $A$, and between $A$ and $E$, we infer that $A$ lies between $D$ and $E$. Let's mark three points $A$, $D$, and $E$ on the straight line:

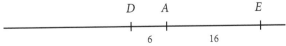

*D* and *C* are 6 miles apart, just like *D* and *A*, hence *C* and *A* must lie on opposite sides of *D*.

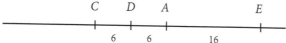

Finally, the distance between *A* and *B* is 16 miles, i.e., the same as between *A* and *E*. We infer that *B* and *E* lie on opposite sides of *A*, while *B* and *C* are 16 – 12 = 4 miles apart.

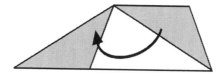

Now we can read out the answer from the graph.

**Answer: The villages in question are located in the following sequence: *BCDAE*, or when driving from the opposite direction, *EADCB*.**

**68.** We divide the trapezoid along one of its diagonals – see figure below.

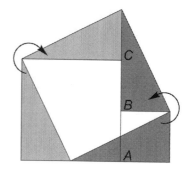

**69.**

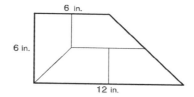

**70.** The way to partition the shape is shown in the provided figure. It might be of some help to calculate the side length of the newly formed square. If the side length of the small square equals 1, then the side length of the big square is 2, i.e., their total area equals 5. Hence the conclusion is that the side length of the square obtained after putting the three shapes together must be $\sqrt{5} = \sqrt{2^2 + 1^2}$ , i.e., the same as the hypotenuse of a right triangle with the sides measuring 1 and 2.

**71.** We denote by $a$ the side length of square I (see figure beside). Then, the side length of square II also equals $a$, so the side length of square III is $a + 2$, and square IV $a + 4$. We also know that the side length of square V equals $2a - 2$, so the side length of square IV is equal to $2a - 4$. Comparing the side length of square IV calculated in two ways, we obtain $a + 4 = 2a - 4$, hence $a = 8$. So the side lengths of the whole rectangle are $3a + 2$ and $3a - 2$. Its area equals, therefore, $(3a + 2)(3a - 2) = 9a^2 - 4 = 9 \times 64 - 4 = 572$.
**Answer: The area of the rectangle is 572 in².**

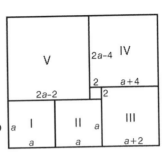

**72.** Pentagon $BCD'EF$ formed of a folded sheet of paper was painted bilaterally, i.e., 24 in² of paper, altogether. After unfolding we have 40 in² of paper (two sides measuring 20 in² each), i.e., the white part takes up $40 - 24 = 16$ in².
**Answer: The area of the white part of the rectangle equals 16 in².**

**73.** The line dividing the perimeter of the square in the ratio of 9:7 and dividing one of the sides (call it side $AB$) in the ratio of 7:1, can cut the square in two ways, depending on whether the longer segment of side $AB$ belongs to the bigger (a) or the smaller (b) part of the square's perimeter (see figure).
In case (b), the line divides the second (left vertical) side of the square in the ratio of 7:1, and not 5:3. This means that the line must run as shown in figure (a). The area of the trapezoid on the left-hand side of the line equals $\frac{8(3+7)}{2} = 40$, and the area of the trapezoid on the right $\frac{8(5+1)}{2} = 24$, i.e., the line divides the area of the square in the ratio of 40:24.

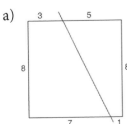

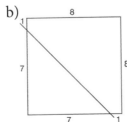

**Answer: The line divides the area of the square in the ratio of 5:3.**

**74.** Let's mark the centers of the circles by $O_1$, $O_2$, $O_3$, $O_4$, and intersection points of the circle with center $O_1$ with circles with centers $O_2$ and $O_4$ by $A$, $B$, $C$, $D$ (see figure). Let's denote by $\alpha$ the magnitude of angle $\sphericalangle AO_1B$. Angles $\sphericalangle BO_1C$ and $\sphericalangle CO_1D$ also have the same $\alpha$ magnitude because they are central angles on the same circle, subtending an arc of the same length (3 in.). Since

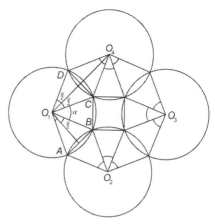

the circles are congruent, and their shorter arcs are of the same length, all the remaining nine angles marked in the figure also have $\alpha$ magnitude. Quadrilateral $O_1AO_2B$ is a rhombus (the length of each of its sides is equal to the radii of the circles), so its diagonal $O_1O_2$ divides angle $\sphericalangle AO_1B$ into two angles of identical magnitude equal to $\frac{\alpha}{2}$. It is just like in the case of rhombus $O_4DO_1C$ and the two remaining ones. Let's now consider quadrilateral $O_1O_2O_3O_4$. The angle at vertex $O_1$ has a magnitude equal to $\frac{\alpha}{2} + \alpha + \frac{\alpha}{2} = 2\alpha$, just as the remaining vertex angles of the quadrilateral. This means that quadrilateral $O_1O_2O_3O_4$ is a square, so $2\alpha = 90°$. Hence the circumference of each circle equals $3 \times \left(\frac{360°}{\alpha}\right) = 3 \times \left(\frac{360°}{45°}\right) = 3 \times 8 = 24$.

**Answer: The circumference of each circle equals 24 in.**

**75.** Arcs $AB$ and $BC$ are of the same length, so $B$ and $C$ are equidistant from the diameter $AD$. Hence segments $BC$ and $AD$ are parallel. Let's mark by $O$ the midpoint of segment $AD$. Triangles $BCA$

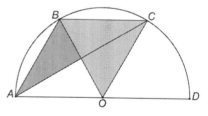

and $BCO$ share a common side: $BC$; the heights of these triangles lowered on this side are of the same length (because $AD$ and $BC$ are parallel). This means that the area of these triangles is the same (see figure below). The area to be found is then equal to the area of the circular sector $BCO$, i.e., $\frac{1}{6}$ of the area of the whole circle. Hence we calculate: $\frac{1}{6} \times 10^2\,\pi = \frac{50\,\pi}{3}$ (in²).

**Answer: The area of the curvilinear triangle ABC equals $\frac{50\,\pi}{3}$ (in²).**

**76.** Since $|PB| + |BQ| = |AB| = |PB| + |AP|$, so $|BQ| = |AP|$. This means that the rectangular triangles $QBA$ and $PAD$ have their respective legs of the same length: $|BQ| = |AP|$ and $|AB| = |AD|$, i.e., they are congruent, hence $|\sphericalangle PAQ| = |\sphericalangle ADP|$. Similarly triangles $PBC$ and $QCD$ are congruent, so $\sphericalangle PCQ| = |\sphericalangle QDC|$. Therefore, $|\sphericalangle PAQ| + |\sphericalangle PDQ| + |\sphericalangle PCQ| = = |\sphericalangle ADP| + |\sphericalangle PDQ| + |\sphericalangle QDC| = |\sphericalangle ADC| = 90°$.

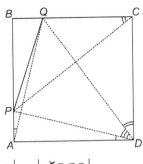

**77.** Let's mark by $G$ the point of contact of the two circles $C_D$ and $C_E$ (see figure). We see that radius $R$ of circle $C_F$ equals $R = |FD| + |DG|$, and on the other side, $R = |FE| + |EG|$. Hence $2R = |FD| + |DG| + + |FE| + |EG| = |FD| + (|DG| + + |EG|) + |FE| = 30$ in, i.e., $R = 15$ in.

**Answer: The radius length of circle $C_F$= 15 in.**

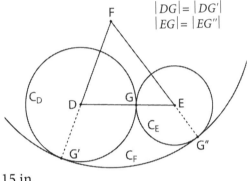

$|DG| = |DG'|$
$|EG| = |EG''|$

**78.** Let's mark by $\alpha$, $\beta$, and $\gamma$ the angles of this triangle. We have by design $\alpha < \beta + \gamma$, hence $2\alpha < \alpha + \beta + \gamma = 180°$, i.e., $\alpha < 90°$. Similarly, we demonstrate that $\beta < 90°$ and $\gamma < 90°$, from which we conclude that this is an acute triangle. If the triangle is acute-angled, then each of its angles is smaller than 90°, so the sum of each of its two angles is greater than 90°. Therefore, each acute triangle satisfies the condition of the problem. This means that for a triangle meeting the condition of the problem, we cannot say anything other than it is acute-angled.

**Answer: This triangle is acute-angled.**

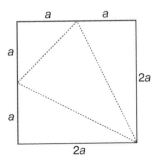

**79.** Yes, it is possible (to obtain a tetrahedron by folding a square sheet of paper along the dotted lines) – see figure beside.

**Answer: Yes, the figure in question can be a square.**

**80.** Let's mark by $E$ and $F$ the midpoints of the sides of square $PQRS$ which is intersecting with square $ABCD$, and by $X$ and $Y$ the intersections of the sides of both squares (see figure below).

Then, angles $\sphericalangle XEA$ and $\sphericalangle YFA$ are right angles, and the magnitudes of angles $\sphericalangle XAE$ and $\sphericalangle YAF$ are equal, because $\sphericalangle XAE = 90° - \sphericalangle EAY = \sphericalangle YAF$.

Moreover, segments $AE$ and $AF$ are equal in length. Therefore, triangles $XAE$ and $YFA$ are congruent by virtue of the rule of congruency (angle-side-angle), and thus they have the same area. So the area of the shaded part equals the area of square $ERFA$, and the area of this square is equal to $\frac{1}{4}$ of the area of square $PQRS$, i.e., $\frac{1}{4} \times 100$ in² $= 25$ in².

**Answer: The common area shared by both $PQRS$ and $ABCD$ squares equals 25 in².**

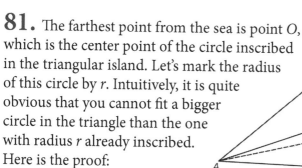

**81.** The farthest point from the sea is point $O$, which is the center point of the circle inscribed in the triangular island. Let's mark the radius of this circle by $r$. Intuitively, it is quite obvious that you cannot fit a bigger circle in the triangle than the one with radius $r$ already inscribed. Here is the proof:

Let's assume that a certain point $S$ within the triangle lies farther from all its sides than point $O$. Let $d_{AB}$, $d_{BC}$, and $d_{AC}$ be the distances of sides $AB$, $BC$, and $CA$ (respectively) from point $S$.

By assumption, $d_{AB} > r$, $d_{BC} > r$ and $d_{AC} > r$.

Then, $P_{\triangle ABC} = P_{\triangle AOB} + P_{\triangle BOC} + P_{\triangle AOC} = \frac{(|AB| \times r + |BC| \times r + |CA| \times r)}{2} =$

$= \frac{(r \times (|AB| + |BC| + |CA|))}{2}$.

On the other side, we also have:

$P_{\triangle ABC} = P_{\triangle ASB} + P_{\triangle BSC} + P_{\triangle ASC} = \frac{(|AB| \times d_{AB} + |BC| \times d_{BC} + |CA| \times d_{AC})}{2} >$

$> \frac{(|AB| \times r + |BC| \times r + |CA| \times r)}{2} = \frac{r \times (|AB| + |BC| + |CA|)}{2}$, which is in contradiction

with the previous equality. This is consequent with the assumption that in triangle *ABC*, there is a point *S* distant from each of the sides of the triangle by more than *r*.

**Answer: The farthest from the sea lies the point which is the center of the circle inscribed in the triangle representing the island.**

**82.** We name *F*, *G*, and *S* additional intersection points on the grid – see figure beside.

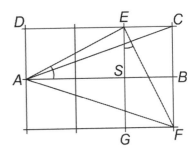

Angles $\sphericalangle BAC$ and $\sphericalangle BAF$ are equal, so

$|\sphericalangle BAC| + |\sphericalangle BAE| = |\sphericalangle BAF| + |\sphericalangle BAE| =$

$= |\sphericalangle EAF|$.

Triangles *ASE* and *EGF* are congruent (they are right triangles, and the lengths of adjacent legs are 1 and 2),

so $|\sphericalangle AEF| = |\sphericalangle AES| + |\sphericalangle GEF| = |\sphericalangle AES| + |\sphericalangle SAE| = 180° - |\sphericalangle ASE| = 90°$.

Moreover, $|AE| = |EF|$, i.e., triangle *AEF* is isosceles, and its vertex angle *E* is a right angle. Therefore, $|\sphericalangle EAF| = 45°$.

**Answer: The sum of angles $\sphericalangle BAC$ and $\sphericalangle BAE$ equals 45°.**

# CHAPTER 5

## GAMES, LOGICAL TESTS AND OTHERS

**83.** It is possible, e.g., Anne Smith (a brunette), Mary Smith (a blonde), Anne Newman (a blonde), and Mary Newman (a brunette).
**Answer: It is possible to satisfy the set conditions.**

**84.** Once the successive layers of the hexahedrons are drawn layer by layer (starting from the layer at the base), we count the cubes – see figures below.

a) – 88 cubes

b) – 70 cubes

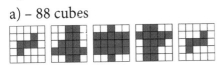
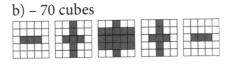

c) – 45 cubes

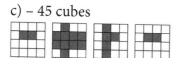

d) – 76 cubes

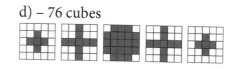

**Answer: The hexahedrons consist of:**
**a) 88 cubes, b) 70 cubes, c) 45 cubes, and d) 76 cubes.**

**85.** Matthew was sitting to the right of Agatha, so Kevin must have been sitting to her left side. To the left of Kevin might have been sitting either Celine or Daphne (we do not take Barbara into account as she is Matthew's wife). Let's consider both cases:

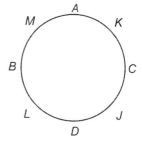

a) If it was Celine sitting to the left of Kevin, then to her left must have been John (Kevin and Matthew are already sitting elsewhere, and Leon is Celine's husband). We know that Daphne was also sitting next to John, so she must have taken a seat to his left. The remaining two seats were occupied by Leon and Barbara (see figure beside), which means that to the right of Barbara was Leon.

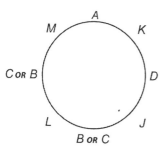

b) If it was Daphne sitting to the left of Kevin, then, per the guidelines of the problem, to her left side sat John. The next three seats were occupied by: Barbara, Celine, and Leon; Leon was sitting between Barbara and Celine (otherwise the two ladies would have been sitting next to each other) – see figure on the left.

In that case, however, Celine would have then been neighboring on her husband, Leon. This case is, therefore, rejected as being impossible.

**Answer: Leon sat to the right of Barbara.**

**86.** We must leave the marks 0 and 11 in., for otherwise it would not be possible to measure out 11 inches with a ruler. Leaving in only the other marks, e.g., $a$, $b$, and $c$ inches, where $a < b < c$, we could measure distances $a$, $b$, $c$, 11, $b - a$, $c - a$, $11 - a$, $c - b$, $11 - b$, and $11 - c$ (some of these distances can be equal), i.e., we could measure ten different distances from 1 to 11 in, at most. Among them there would be at least one integer-type distance from 1 to 11 in, which could not be measured. That is why we need to leave in at least four marks, apart from the two denoting 1 and 11 in.

Such a ruler can easily be found using a trial and error method:

**Answer: You can remove six marks, at most.**

**87.** Let's assume that Dorothy is telling lies. Then, the remaining girls would be telling the truth, and none of them would be the youngest, which is, of course, impossible. It is Dorothy, then, who is telling the truth, and she really is the youngest.

If Annie is telling the truth, then she is the eldest, but that would mean that all the girls are telling the truth, which is in contradiction with the conditions stated in the problem. So it is Annie who is lying, and the remaining girls are telling the truth. Hence we conclude that the eldest is Celine.

**Answer: Dorothy is the youngest, and Celine is the eldest.**

**88.** Since the inhabitants of each village begin their conversation with a true sentence, the information in the first sentence said by the caller notifying the fire brigade of the fire is true. Let's check all the possibilities:

a) If the caller was from Aden, then all his answers are true. It would follow from the second sentence that the fire had broken out in Aden, whereas from the third, that the village of Caden was on fire. This is of course impossible, because the fire had broken out in only one village.

b) If the call was from Baden, then from the second answer, we conclude that no fire had broken out either in Baden or Caden (answer 3). So the fire must have broken out in Aden.

c) If the call was made by an inhabitant of Caden, then we know from the second answer that the fire had started in some other village than Caden; however, from the third answer, it follows that Caden was on fire, which is a blatant contradiction.

**Answer: The fire was reported by an inhabitant of Baden. The duty officer should direct the fire engine to Aden.**

**89.** The gang boss is not standing next to Julian. If this was the case, then Julian would have told a lie only once, while answering question 2 or 3. So neither John nor Igor can be the gang leader. Julian is not the boss either; if he were, he would have then given four false answers. Neither is James the gang boss, for if he were, he would not have told a lie even once. Last but not least, Peter cannot be the boss either, because if he were, he would have given false answers to the first three questions. However, if David is not the boss, then among the six captured criminals would not have been their leader, but in that case Julian would have given false answers to the last three questions, which is not true. It is clear then that David is the boss.
**Answer: David is the gang leader.**


**90.** It is not true. For instance, in the set 1, 2, 3, 4, 5, and 10, there are no such two numbers whose sum or difference is divisible by 10.
*Note: If there were seven numbers, the answer would be affirmative. In fact, if among them are two numbers ending with the same digit, then their difference ends with a zero, i.e., their difference is divisible by 10. Let's assume that these numbers end with various digits. At the very most, two of them can end with digits 0 or 5, so at least five numbers will end with a digit from the set {1, 2, 3, 4, 6, 7, 8, and 9}. Let's divide this set of digits into four subsets: {1, 9}, {2, 8}, {3, 7}, and {4, 6}. Since there are at least five numbers, and they end with different digits, this means that some two numbers end with digits belonging to the same (two-element) subset of numbers. The sum of these two numbers ends with zero, so it is divisible by 10.*


**91.** It is enough to take out a ball from the box marked (W, G). In this box, due to Anne's carelessness, there are balls of the same color; there are two possibilities, then:
a) In the box marked (W, G), there are two white balls. In that case, a pair of green balls is in the box marked (W, W) – they cannot be in the (G, G) box, because in such a case they would be in their right place – and the two-color ones in the box marked (G, G).
b) In the box marked (W, G), there are two green balls. In that case, the pair of white balls is in the (G, G) box, while the white ball with the green one are in the (W, W) box.

**92.** We have: $300 = 100 + 100 + 100 = (a_1 + a_2 + a_3 + \ldots + a_{50}) +$
$+ (a_1 + a_2 + a_3 + \ldots + a_{50}) + (a_1 + a_2 + a_3 + \ldots + a_{50}) = (a_1 + a_2 + a_3) +$
$+ (a_4 + a_5 + a_6) + \ldots + (a_{46} + a_{47} + a_{48}) + (a_{49} + a_{50} + a_1) + (a_2 + a_3 + a_4) +$
$+ \ldots + (a_{47} + a_{48} + a_{49}) + (a_{50} + a_1 + a_2) + (a_3 + a_4 + a_5) + \ldots +$
$+ (a_{48} + a_{49} + a_{49})$.

On the right-hand side, there are 50 elements (each of them being the sum of three numbers). If each of the terms was smaller than 6, their sum would be smaller than $50 \times 6 = 300$, so it would not equal 300. Therefore, one of the terms equals at least 6. The term is, of course, the sum of three numbers among $a_1$, $a_2$, $a_3$, …, and $a_{50}$.

**Answer: Yes, there must be three such numbers.**

**93.** In the basket, there cannot be 12 mushrooms other than ceps – choosing any 12 mushrooms, we would not find a cep among them. Therefore, there may be no more than 11 mushrooms other than ceps in the basket. Hence we conclude that there are at least 30 – 11 = 19 ceps. Thinking along the same lines, the basket cannot contain 20 mushrooms other than brown ring boletuses, and picking out 20 mushrooms, we must find at least one brown ring boletus among them. So there can only be at most 19 mushrooms other than brown ring boletuses in the basket, hence the conclusion that there are at least 30 – 19 = 11 brown ring boletuses in the basket.

There are 30 mushrooms altogether. Among them there are at least 19 ceps and at least 11 brown ring boletuses; hence we know that the girls have gathered 19 ceps and 11 brown ring boletuses.

**Answer: There are 19 ceps in the basket.**

**94.** After drawing 25 balls, we will be left with 5 balls in the box. If we take 25 balls out of the box in such a way that all the remaining ones will be white, among the 25 drawn ones will be at least three white balls. Therefore, there are at least 5 + 3 = 8 white balls. (It is of course possible to draw 25 balls in such a way as to have only white ones left in the box, because if there were fewer than five white balls, it might happen that all of them would remain in the box, and then, among the 25 balls drawn, there would be no single white one).

Similarly, there are at least 5 + 5 = 10 blue balls and 5 + 7 = 12 black ones.

Since 8 + 10 + 12 = 30, this means that there are 8 white balls, 10 blue balls, and 12 black ones.

**Answer: There are 8 white balls, 10 blue balls, and 12 black ones.**

**95.** From one point, be it *A*, come out five segments.

Among them are at least three having the same color, e.g., blue. Let's mark the ends of these segments by *B*, *C*, and *D*. If any of the segments *BC*, *CD*, or *DB* happens to be blue (e.g., *BC*), we will obtain a triangle with blue sides (in our example, this will be triangle *ABC*). If, however, all three segments *BC*, *CD*, and *DB* are red, then triangle *BCD* has all its sides red. This means that the newly formed triangle will have its sides in the same color.

**Answer: Sophie did not perform her task and did not receive the prize.**

**96.** Let's mark the glasses with arrows: ↑ will denote a glass standing stem side up, while ↓ will mean a glass standing stem side down. The initial line-up was as follows: ↑↓↑↓↑. The first player will win if he/she turns glass 5. It will lead to the following arrangement: ↑↓↑↓↓. Now the second player has three possible moves:

a) and b) To turn one of the two ↑ glasses, but then the other player may win instantly, turning the remaining ↑ glass.

c) To turn glasses number 2 and 3, leading to the line-up ↑↑↓↓↓. Again the first player wins, turning glasses number 1 and 2.

**Answer: Yes, the person starting the game can always win.**

**97.** By writing the digit 8, the first player forces the second to write the digit 9. Therefore, the first player can keep on writing an 8, compelling the second to the 9 – as a result the players will form the following number 898,989,898,989. The sum of the digits of the number equals $6 \times 8 + 6 \times 9 = 6 \times 17$ and is divisible by 3, i.e., the newly formed number is also divisible by 3. So the person beginning the game will always win by writing an 8.

*Note: It can be proven that the player beginning the game with a digit other than an 8 will invariably lose (if of course his/her opponent takes advantage of it).*

**Answer: The person beginning the game has a winning strategy.**

**98.** It would be worth considering the final moments of the game. When one of the players writes a number from 90 to 99, the second one can win at once, writing 100. So if one of the boys writes 89, his opponent must add a number found in the range of 90 and 99, after which, as we already know, the first contender is going to win. Thus, writing the number 89 = 100 − 11 guarantees a victory.

Similarly, if one player chooses the number 78 = 89 − 11, he automatically compels his opponent to pick a number from 79 to 88, and by doing so wins after writing 89. In other words, the choice of the number 78 ensures (with a proper strategy adopted, that is) a win. In order to win, it is enough to always write numbers different from 100 by a certain multiple of 11. That is why Adam, who begins, will win, if − in his first move − he writes the number 1 (= 100 − 9 × 11), and in his next moves, he chooses the numbers 12, 23, 34, 45, 56, 67, 78, 89, and 100. He will always be able to write them, irrespective of what his opponent does.

**Answer: The starter always has a winning strategy – in order to win he should begin with the number 1, and then successively 12, 23, 34, 45, 56, 67, 78, 89, and 100.**

**99.** Apparently, the game will end with the victory of one of the players, because the number of matches in the box decreases with each move.

Let's call the position in the game a position of type *D* where the number of matches in the box is divisible by 3. All other positions will be denoted by *I*. Please note that in a position of type *D* it is impossible to win in one go, for one cannot take out of the box a number of matches divisible by 3.

Each move in the game from a position of type *D* leads to a position of type *I*. Moreover, from position *I*, one can reach position *D* in one go, taking out one or two matchsticks and leaving in the box a number of matches divisible by 3.

a) If the initial number of matches in the box is 48, Player 2 has a winning strategy. The initial position is of type *D*, so after whichever move Player 1 makes, it changes into the position of type *I*. Now Player 2 reinstates position *D*, etc. Player 1 must, with every move he makes, restore position *I*, to which Player 2 responds with a move that brings back position *D*. With such a strategy adopted by Player 2, the first one will never win, because he always makes moves in position *D*, and as we have already established, one cannot win in one go moving from this position. Since the game ends with the win of one competitor, the winner will be Player 2.

b) If the box initially contains 49 matches, Player 1 will win by taking out one matchstick and using the strategy described in point a) since Player 2 will be making his first move with 48 matches in the box. As we have shown above, this is a losing position.

**Answer: If there are 48 matches in the box, Player 1 has no winning strategy. If, however, the box contains 49 matchsticks, the starter does have a winning strategy – he should take out but one matchstick.**

**100.** Mark will win if he puts the first tile on squares 4 and 5 (or symmetrically on squares 9 and 10). Then, the tape will be divided into two parts – the left-hand one will fit exactly one tile, regardless of what the players do:

| 1 | 2 | 3 | 4 | 5 | 6 | 7 | 8 | 9 | 10 | 11 | 12 | 13 |
|---|---|---|---|---|---|---|---|---|----|----|----|----|

In his second move, Mark must make sure that just three tiles can fit in the right-hand part – then he will win. He can, for instance, proceed as follows:

a) If Daniel leaves squares 9 and 10 free (e.g., he puts the tile on squares 12 and 13), Mark will in his second move put the tile on squares 9 and 10. There will remain free spots for two tiles: One will be taken by Daniel, and the other, by Mark, thanks to which he will win:

| 1 | 2 | 3 | 4 | 5 | 6 | 7 | 8 | 9 | 10 | 11 | 12 | 13 |
|---|---|---|---|---|---|---|---|---|----|----|----|----|

b) If Daniel puts the tile on spots 8 and 9 (or 10 and 11), Mark will cover squares 11 and 12 (or 7 and 8). Again there will remain empty spots for two tiles, so Mark will win once more:

| 1 | 2 | 3 | 4 | 5 | 6 | 7 | 8 | 9 | 10 | 11 | 12 | 13 |
|---|---|---|---|---|---|---|---|---|----|----|----|----|

c) If Daniel covers squares 9 and 10, there will remain enough room for three tiles.

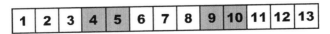

Mark can now put the tile on any free square – he will win no matter what Daniel does. If the tape consisted of 14 squares, Mark would also have a winning strategy. It would suffice if he put the first tile on the two central spots.

From now on, he should place the tiles symmetrically to Daniel's moves. For example, if Daniel were to put a tile on squares 2 and 3, Mark would cover squares 12 and 13:

Playing in this way, Mark will always be able respond to Daniel's move, so as not to lose. Since the game ends when all the empty spots have been covered, someone must lose, and this will be Daniel.

**Answer: In both cases Mark, who begins the game, has a winning strategy.**

Made in the USA
Lexington, KY
10 November 2014